TALES *of* PRIUT ALMUS

Participant Observation in a Russian Children's Shelter

Robert Belenky

iUniverse, Inc.
New York   Bloomington

Tales of Priut Almus
Participant Observation in a Russian Children's Shelter

iUniverse books may be ordered through booksellers or by contacting:

iUniverse
1663 Liberty Drive
Bloomington, IN 47403
www.iuniverse.com
1-800-Authors (1-800-288-4677)

Because of the dynamic nature of the Internet, any Web addresses or links contained in this book may have changed since publication and may no longer be valid. The views expressed in this work are solely those of the author and do not necessarily reflect the views of the publisher, and the publisher hereby disclaims any responsibility for them.

ISBN: 978-1-4401-3151-6 (pbk)
ISBN: 978-1-4401-3153-0 (cloth)
ISBN: 978-1-4401-3152-3 (ebk)

Printed in the United States of America

iUniverse rev. date: 4/21/09

Contents

Preface

Tales of Almus is the fifth in a series of books by Robert Belenky about raising children whose lives have not been easy.

The first, *Fragments of a Lesson Plan*, (Beacon, 1971; iUniverse, 2003), provides the reader a close-up view of a parent-run, fully integrated, after-school program for children in a racially divided Boston housing project. In the second, *La Chanson de Chanmas,* (Booksurge, 2004), eight girls who live in a park in Port-au-Prince, Haiti, reflect movingly on their lives. It is written in three languages, Haitian Creole, French and English. The third, Наш Дом/*Our House*, (Booksurge, 2005), including both English and Russian versions, brings the reader into a Russian boarding school through observations, interviews and anecdotes. All are available at *amazon. com, barnesandnoble.com*, and *borders.com*.

A fourth book, *Camaraderie,* (XLibris, 2004) may be ordered at *xlibris.com*. It is an album of photographs of Haitian and Russian children introduced by the children's own words.

More books are planned in this series.

Acknowledgements

This book is dedicated to the children of Priut Almus.

It could never have been written without the support of

- Mikhail Makarievich and his gracious staff.

- My mentor and friend Dr. Alla Pavlovna Suroteva.

- Jeff Groton, my first boss and teacher at Doctors of the World, St. Petersburg

- Dr. Roman Vladimirovich Yorik and his colleagues, past and present, at Doctors of the World, St. Petersburg.

- Mary Whalen's 2008 graduating class from Vermont's Twinfield High School for reading an early draft of this book and assuring me that it is as interesting to teenagers as I hoped it would be.

- Blythe and Evans Clinchy for their helpful comments on an early manuscript draft.

- Vera Bade for her help in translation and for her understanding of Russia.

- Andy Doe, man of the theater, for his critique of this book fueled by his love of A.P. Chekhov.

- Rochelle Ruthchild for her detailed critique, scholarly insights and cultural knowledge.

- My family: Mary, my wife, the most sensible and persuasive of critics and the best lifetime friend a person could imagine. Sophie and Max, my parents, long since gone. My adult children, Alice and Michael, and my teenage grandchildren, Sofia, Ella, Max, Oliver and Simon.

- Many others also helped bring *Tales of Almus* to fruition including all those mentioned in the text, children and adults alike. My apologies to those I may have inadvertently overlooked.

I am deeply grateful to all of you.

Bob

The Author

Robert Belenky holds a PhD in Clinical Psychology from Teachers College, Columbia University. He earned a USPHS post doctoral fellowship in Child and Family Psychology at the Judge Baker Child Guidance Clinic of the Boston Children's Hospital. He taught at the Harvard Graduate School of Education, Boston College, Boston University, Concordia University, The New School in New York, and was the founding dean of Goddard College's innovative Graduate Program.

He was employed by the Newton, Massachusetts, Public Schools and the Massachusetts Mental Health Center. He spent many years in independent practice and did volunteer work in the US and overseas.

He writes,

My mother was a kindergarten teacher who was trained in the progressive education tradition. My father, born in Russia, emigrated to the US well before the Revolution but returned to Russia on three occasions during the 1920s as head of a tractor team. His job was to train Jewish collective farm settlers in the uses of tractors.

I grew up in New York's Greenwich Village. My parents owned a gift store, the Russian Yarmarka, bursting with with color and exotic toys. I loved to hang out there.

At age five, my parents enrolled me in the laboratory kindergarten of Bank Street College. From then on, it was progressive education all the way except for a stint at a couple of conventional universities.

I enjoyed growing up. I was safe, well fed, loved, educated, and entertained.

Watching the lives of others unfold became my hobby and facilitating their growth, my vocation.

My career began at age thirteen when I found a job as counselor-in-training in an educationally sophisticated, folklore oriented children's camp. I have worked with children ever since in schools, clinics, hospitals, courts, and an independent practice in a forest retreat.

Introduction

I once thought I understood "family" but what I saw then was a chimera. It was only that rare and fortunate family with food on the table, a roof overhead, and a warm hearth; a scene clouded only by interpersonal woe. I knew nothing of family's more frequent embodiment which is the very absence of family. It is a chronic condition of unfulfilled needs; of children huddled under railway station platforms, of orphans abandoned to fate, of victimization by war, disease, and abuse, of derelicts, scroungers, vagabonds, thieves, and crooks who inspire only revulsion in our hearts.

Spread before me was an exotic and perversely attractive netherland, a twilight world yet one consistent with my radical vision of that still untested reality where my assistance might be needed. It teemed with surplus children, ignored by decent people except when their comfort is threatened. These are the neglected, the unseen, the great and not so great unwashed. Police and shopkeepers tidy the streets each morning by gunning them down for sport as they sleep under the marquee of an abandoned movie theater.

My interest was both romantic and professional. I

wanted to know how such children survive. I wanted to know what if anything was being done for them. I was eager to help.

I became preoccupied with the question of what we, citizens of good will, well fed, well meaning, ambiguously motivated people, might offer such children. We *are,* of course, obligated to do something, are we not?

More than anything, I was curious. I wanted simply to meet the kids, see them, hear them, talk with them and, as no more than a journalist, to obtain some sense of what their lives are like. Then, who knows, I might even consider … taking arms against a sea of troubles.

I admit to coming to this equipped with prejudices. First was that neither police power nor traditional institutions are likely to be of much help. Second, that neither foster care nor adoption are the answer except for the very rare luck of the draw.

- - - - - - - - - - - - - - - -

Was this to be another academic study? Was there a coherent argument to be made? A goal? A purpose? No. Probably not. Rather, my intent was personal. The process was its purpose. I have always worked with children, usually with those who were having problems with their families. But seldom did I get to know unwanted, bargain-basement children who had no families at all, children who, an overstocked commodity especially in hard times, are a glut on the market. I looked forward to meeting those surplus children, coming to know them, cracking jokes with them and just horsing around with them. At first I had little sense of what I was doing but gradually I learned a few simple lessons from those rare, skilled, self-sacrificing teachers and counselors who make a positive difference in the lives of such children.

I retired over a dozen years ago and began at once to make annual visits to Haiti and Russia to acquaint myself with children of the streets and those who live in institutions. For each subsequent year I returned to the same countries, the same programs, the same institutions and, where possible, the same children. I was searching for a method, an attitude, a way to relate, an alchemy to transform lives.

- - - - - - - - - - - - - - - -

Why Russia? Well, access was easy. I had good contacts, not-so-distant relatives, and I persuaded myself that since Russian history and traditions are unlike our own, the potential for discovery was considerable. In summary,

- There are many orphans and abandoned children in Russia.

- The field of mental health in Russia when I began the study was beholden neither to psychodynamics nor to psychopharmacology. Although psychologists and psychiatrists were to be found working in many Russian children's institutions, their approach for the most part appeared to vary between two poles, the white-coated "scientific" and the indulgent-yet-demanding maternal. Freud and his descendants had only just found their way there. Finally, the use of behavioral techniques, although having had a rich history in Russia, did not seem to be present in schools and institutions at the level that we see in the States.

- Residential institutions for children in Russia do not generally aim to cure. They interpret their mandate in a more utilitarian light. Children's failings, while recognized, are taken as givens. Implicitly, the job of the facility is merely to house, clothe, feed and, in some instances, to train the residents in some basic trade. It is at best a benign formulation, a blank slate on which a creative educator can etch impressive structures. In America by contrast we take it as axiomatic that within each child lurks an ailment for which a diagnosis and a proper treatment may be found listed in the Diagnostic and Statistical Manual. Cure is our goal even though we do not know how to achieve it. Thus the optimistic American belief that change is possible, while laudatory, limits our capacity to entertain alternative narratives.

- Russia remains influenced by older ways of thinking about family and community. Side by side with an ancient reverence for family, whether nuclear or extended, one finds traces of the point of view assumed by Soviet educators,[1] that the state is somehow better equipped to raise children than is any version of family. By contrast, faith in the collective is absent in the bones of Americans.

- In our country is it assumed that a child "belongs" to the parent. Property rights come into play. In Russia, however, responsibility is shared with the extended family, indeed with the entire community.

---

1   Anton Makarenko, *Collected Works in Seven Volumes*, 2nd ed., Moscow, 1957.

- Finally, despite our differences, Russia is not an exotic country.   There are oceans of similarity between us. We can recognize, each in the other, a familiar irreverent humor, a careless audacity, a rough-edged shrewdness, and a frontier wit often expressed with macho exuberance.   It was thus my hope that what I would learn in Russia could be applicable at once in the United States.

Shelters for children existed in Russia during the time of the tsars but they were discontinued under the Soviets in favor of boarding schools and orphanages, most of them soulless and authoritarian. After the demise of the Soviet Union, shelters reappeared on the scene. Because of the openness of the design and their potential for the empowerment of children, they attracted the interest of some highly creative Russian educators along with the nervous distrust of the authorities.

Priut Almus—"The Almus Children's Shelter"—is a splendid post-Soviet conception, humane, spirited, creative yet, in its own way, disciplined and determined to prepare children to live in a democracy. It is unique in that it is based philosophically more in theater than in pedagogy. Its founder-director, Mikhail Makarievich— actor, director, stage manager, loose cannon—is a powerful advocate for young people.

This book chronicles what I experienced during visits to Pruit Almus over a period of some ten years. The first three were as volunteer consultant to the US office of Doctors of the World, Almus' sponsoring organization. The remaining ones were made on my own initiative,

I began in optimism. I could barely speak the Russian language (shamefully, I have advanced only modestly since then) and I had only the most general notion of what I was to do. Bravely, I threw myself into the fray, living in Almus for days, even weeks, at a time although after a while, starting with the fourth year, my visits were reduced to check-ins lasting no more than a few hours. My computer disk was soon overflowing with notes, photographs and impressions.

It surprisingly became evident that my ignorance was an advantage of sorts. I had no choice but to present myself as an outsider, well-meaning but uncomprehending, a man from Mars. I was reduced to observing, listening and absorbing the scene that played out around me as best I could. I was deaf but not blind. It was better, I realized, to limit stimuli and to be free of the burdens of role and purpose.

Moreover, incompetence in the language put children at a pleasing advantage. They knew what I, the adult, did not know and so of necessity they became my teachers. The possibility of my comprehending their language and their society required their assistance. Even now, as images stabilize and come into focus and early clues lead to discovery, I remain grateful to them.

- - - - - - - - - - - - - - - -

Allow me to introduce you to a Russian kid.

Hello. My name is Sergei[2] but you may call me Serogia. I am thirteen. How did I get to Priut Almus? Well, I was thrown out of my house. You see, I was living with my mother and my father. Well, they weren't actually

---

2   Sometimes children's first names and nicknames are disguised in this book. Family names are never used. A few place names have been changed as well.

my mother and father. They were just people who were raising me. Then my father died. I hated my mother and didn't ever do anything she wanted me to do. She was a drunk. But I liked my father and always did everything he asked. After he died, my mother didn't know what to do with me.

My real parents couldn't raise me because they lost their parental rights. My real mother was a drunk and I lost my father. I mean he ran away. I don't have any idea where he is. From the time I was three until I was five, I lived in a dom rebyonok (a "baby home," an orphanage for infants).

I visit my grandmother on weekends. I see my brother there. He lives with her. He is sixteen.

I don't remember what the dom rebyonok was like but I know that such places are usually bad.

I've been here at Almus for two months. Next summer I will live in an internat (boarding school) for boys where they learn to be sailors. I tried to get in there before— three times. The first time they only took children without families and I had a family so I wasn't eligible. The second time I didn't show up at the exams and the third time, they had no place for me. But I will try again. I will make it sooner or later.

I want to be a sailor because my grandfather was a sailor. From when I was born until the time I was three, I lived with my grandfather in the city of Nezhni Novgorod. It was my grandfather who put me in the dom rebyonok. Then my grandfather died. I was very sad because he was a good man and nice to me.

When I grow up, I will get married and have children.

I will be a good father. A good father takes care of his children. I will not drink because I do not want to be like my father who left us—he was a drunk. Or like my mother who is now in prison. They put her there because she killed her boyfriend.

I like school. I am a good student. When I was in the first grade, I had a computer so everyone thought I was some kind of genius. But I didn't go to school for a while because I was sick and after that there were holidays. And I lived in the Voskreseniya Dietskiy Priut *(The Sunday Children's Shelter) for one month. So I fell way behind.*

At Voskreseniya they made me believe in God and made me pray before I did anything. There wasn't actually a director there. There was just this banker guy who owned the place. But I didn't like it because they didn't let me go to school. They said school is evil because it's dirty. According to them, everything outside their stupid priut is evil and dirty.

They didn't want me to be a sailor. They said that God doesn't like sailors. They think He doesn't like anything except their stupid priut. I believe in God but not in their kind of thing.

Almus is okay because here people think about my future. Just this morning I was talking about my future with a vospitatel *(male child care worker). He will help me become a sailor.*

- - - - - - - - - - - - - - - -

Given a kid like that, how might I proceed? What are my options? Perhaps, I thought, I shall become a mirror into which children may see their best selves. Or perhaps I shall be a big man and demonstrate solidarity (which is no small thing). Perhaps I shall simply look the child straight in the eye and generate in both of us a spark of recognition. Maybe I should be a parent which is something that is sorely needed but well beyond my willingness and capacity. Or a grandpa. Why not a grandpa? No matter what I choose to become, I must articulate boundaries, remember the limits and never advertise more than I can deliver.

There is a temptation to take on all woes and thus to feed the ego.

So what did I finally become? A friend from a distant land, an entertainer, a bumbling grandpa, out to adopt institutions and programs but never individual children even the sweetest and saddest among them.

Right away, they called me "Grandpa." Better Grandpa than Pa, of course. Pa is a constant, loving supplier of life's necessities. But Grandpa is only an occasional presence, a cheerful, doting, less than responsible fool who is never in charge. Expectations for grandfathers are blessedly low.

It is best, I have come to believe, for the would-be helper, the foreigner especially, to stand at sufficient remove to see the child in full context including the institution, the program, and the family (if indeed there is one) and then humbly to remain there, an eternal, benign fantasy.

1998

It is evening, a quarter to nine. I am sitting at the table of my tiny apartment in Priut Almus, somewhere in St. Petersburg. We drove a long way from center city to get here and took many turns. It is much like being in Brooklyn or Queens but less exotic. This is to be my home for two weeks.

Almus is located in a former child care center. It later became a Soviet-style communal apartment, a "*komumalka*." Now it is a children's shelter. "Priut" means shelter in Russian. The long, two-story, brick-walled building is situated in the midst of a towering public housing complex. Each building has a white, concrete facade, now crumbling. Yet the project is not particularly old, twenty years at most.

The Almus structure is, I suspect, newer than the apartment high-rises, as cheaply built but probably in better repair. It is only two stories tall. The kitchen and dining room are on the ground floor along with a medical clinic for the residents. An after-school program was added recently. It is also on the ground floor. The children's dorm rooms are upstairs.

I ring the bell. The concierge unlocks the door. *"Dobroy dyen,"* good day, he says. I climb the stairs and find myself on the dormitory floor. Children's drawings are arranged on the walls. There is none of the musty odor common in such places, smells that emanate from the brew of sweat, pee and the debris of active lives. Almus is clean yet informal. Hardly pristine, it is well lived in.

The dormitory is divided by a corridor that extends to the far wall in either direction. Children are seen racing cheerfully from one end to the other for no apparent reason. Rooms with two to four beds each line both sides of the hallway. At the center is a small gathering place complete with sofa and chairs. Adjacent is the staff office. The staff kitchen is a few doors away just beyond which is a room large enough for children and staff to meet together.

I am offered a guest suite that doubles as a storeroom. I am delighted to find adequate space for small-group conversations as well as a functioning bathroom complete with a knee-high water pipe useful as a shower. The bed is narrow but firm and comfortable. The bedroom contains a white, Danish-style wardrobe. The walls are adorned with plain, white wallpaper. Crumbling plaster is nowhere to be seen.

Children live in tidy, two-person rooms. Although privacy for them is unlikely, in the generous quarters given to me there is surprising potential for being alone. The door even has a lock that works with a key both from the inside and the outside. Luxury!

I am a mental health consultant to Doctors of the World ("*Vrachi Mira*"), Priut Almus' sponsor. I do not know what they expect. What *is* a psychologist anyway according to their understanding? How do they suppose that he or she might be helpful?

My plan is to learn about the children, the program, and see what may be needed. Although I am to serve Almus in some way, I intend to take something of Russian child-care wisdom and craft back home with me. In that I am the opposite of a missionary. I am not here to sell my god - although I do tend to push progressive education and I extol the virtues of electronic cameras and computers. More to the point is that even with a doctorate, I am hardly a doctor incapable as I am of curing anybody of anything including malaise of the soul.

Perhaps as I sink into the scene, I will find ways to be useful and might even acquire a smattering of the unfathomable Russian language.

This, by the way, is not the first children's institution in Russia that I have come to know. It is the third.

Priut Almus was recommended to me by Vrachi Mira as unusually convivial and innovative. A certain Mikhail Makarievich is the founder and director. He is, I am told, a great but oddball educator.

- - - - - - - - - - - - - - - - -

Dinner: Along with the kids and staff, I devoured a stewed chicken dinner. It was simple food but tasty and more than ample.

The evening consisted of horsing around with children in the playroom, punching, wrestling and giggling. Eventually I stretched out on the sofa in front of the television set, surrounded by kids, all of us staring at the screen, oblivious, transfixed by nothing in particular. Now and then a staff member strolled by and smiled benignly.   There seemed to be no objection to our roughhouse.

I padded off to bed.

As I write this, children remain zoned out at the TV.

- - - - - - - - - - - - - - - -

Nobody speaks English here so I have not benefitted from formal introductions.   Dr. Alla Pavlovna, Vrachi Mira's director of medicine, drove me and stayed for a while. Her command of English is slightly better than mine is of Russian. Thanks to her, I managed to learn a few things.

There are only eighteen children in residence just now. The capacity is thirty or more especially with doubling-up in the rooms.   Ages can range widely from three or four to about eighteen. There is much coming and going on almost a daily basis. Children may stay here for a few days or as long as a year but, by law, no more. Some do remain longer because Makarich is good at arguing their cases with the powers that be.

The director, Mikail Makarievich, "Makarich," is in hospital just now with a broken leg. Alla tells me that he is a remarkable man. I am not sure how he earned that reputation but I shall find out. It is unfortunate that he will not be here. Perhaps I can visit him in hospital or schedule another visit for next year if I return.

This feels like a fine place. It is well staffed with pleasant people ... although a moment ago a big guy patrolling the halls yelled at a bunch of the children. Maybe it was justified but his manner was distinctly grouchy.

On the other hand, I noticed an earnest *vospitatilnitsa* (female child care worker) in the television room surrounded by a throng of children. She strummed a guitar, leading them in song. If she is representative of staff quality, I expect the ambience here to be marked by high spirits and warmheartedness.

Almus stands in stark contrast with the priut for abused children I was taken to yesterday. That place struck me as coldly professional, entirely lacking in homeyness. Here there seems to be much animated interaction between staff and children. Alla Pavlovna hugged bunches of kids at once as we walked in the door.

But there are a few forebodings of concerns. Far be it for me to dwell on them, but did I imagine a whiff of alcohol somewhere along the second floor corridor? Well, I did for certain notice the younger of the two Serogias race down the hall followed by a pack of friends, all giggling and yelling as he waved lit matches in the faces of everyone he passed and then thrust them, flaming, into his mouth.

And, as one of the boys showed me around the facility and along the way invited us into his room, did I imagine the embarrassment in the three boys who stood there awkwardly, the youngest of whom must have been eight or nine years old? It was he who hastily pulled up his pants while the other two guys, a couple of years older, faced him at very close range. What was going on?

There is no question that two thirteen-year-olds, a boy and a girl, strolled from one end of the hallway to the other holding hands—hardly a crime—but it *did* make me wonder about the management problems it must signify in a coed dormitory. Finally, no one could possibly ignore the yelling and running through the corridors after bedtime. Is this place a bit too open, too free, too loosey-goosey?

Well, okay, control may be a bit on the loose side but can civilized behavior really be expected given the population, the circumstances, to say nothing of the history of Russian authoritarianism from which I imagine young people today must feel the need to liberate themselves? Whatever the reasons, I don't envy anyone attempting to run a double-mix residence hall containing boys and girls, adolescents and little kids.

Alla Pavlovna opined that younger children are especially well suited here and happy, too. The program, she said, was designed with them in mind. On the other hand, there are many older kids with serious drug and alcohol problems. This may not be the place for them. What would be? A hospital? A dungeon?

- - - - - - - - - - - - - - - - -

Almus is to be home for the next couple of weeks. Just before bedtime, I invited a few children to play computer games in my kitchen which is also my sitting room. They accepted with enthusiasm. From then on it was never easy to get rid of them.

- - - - - - - - - - - - - - - - -

I slept well last night. The bed was comfortable and I was utterly zonked. It is now a quarter past 9 AM. I need a coffee fix. Russia is a tea-drinking country. My luck. I was told that breakfast would be at nine. There is no sign of it yet. Kids are running this way and that up and down the hallway, most of them still in their pajamas. A *vospitatilnitsa* (female child care worker) announces, "Breakfast in fifteen minutes."

A boy, seven or eight years old: "Please! May I play computer games *now*?"

"After breakfast," I say.

- - - - - - - - - - - - - - - - -

11:30 AM. For the past two hours countless children have wandered in and out of my room. They are pounding on my computer as I write. For the most part they are reasonably well behaved.

"Five minutes more!" I intone.

They know I don't mean it; they play on. That is fine with me because my real goal is to study them. For them to see me as a harmless old coot is to my advantage. They will trust me. When eventually I interview them with the assistance of a translator, I anticipate that their words and thoughts will pour forth comfortably, honestly and spontaneously. From the very soul ... the famous Russian Soul.

As I finally ushered each kid out the door, he or she was immediately replaced by a clone popping in at the door and a new racing, dancing, canny child requesting access to the laptop.

Besides the computer, there was other good stuff in my now-famous sitting room. At her request, I lent Anya my Russian-English/English-Russian dictionary that she had not a clue how to use. She flipped through it nonetheless, feigning competence. Then she handed it back with a cheery "tsank you!" in English. I replied with an equally cheery "*nye za shoto!*" in my best Russian. It means, "No big deal."

- - - - - - - - - - - - - - - - -

Anya, age eleven, is an Alpha Girl. She gets to things first. She was the first to greet me when I arrived and the first to decide which computer games were to be played in my kitchen. She managed to take the first turn on all of them.

Anya sits in the middle of whatever group she is with and may often be seen leading her friends in a foot race from one end of the corridor to the other. Fortunately, she is good-natured and comes across as cheery rather than dictatorial. She is perfectly willing to give a turn to others—once she has had hers. The other kids do more than tolerate her; they appreciate her. I do, too.

Anya and Sasha hang out together. I suspect that they are sisters although they don't look much alike. Anya is ten years old and blond. Sasha is eleven, has dark hair, and is shorter. I had assumed that she was the younger of the two. She is less agile socially and has a partially crossed eye which gives her a bedraggled look. She is the sort of kid I have seen begging for rubles on the St. Petersburg Metro. A sad kid.

Sasha giggles nervously when I look at her. Although she thrives on being noticed, she is skittish. Once when I patted her head, she fled the room but returned a couple of minutes later. Though emotionally hungry, she is easily overwhelmed.

Anya has a wandering eye, too, but it is less pronounced than Sasha's. Anya is much more outgoing and far more talkative. She also loves attention but, unlike her sister, can handle great quantities of it at once. Anya is a leader, not just of kids her own age but of older ones, too.

Later: A vospitatilnitsa informed me that there are in fact two sets of siblings in residence: The dark Anya and Alicia are sisters as are the blond Anya and the female Sasha. Noted.

- - - - - - - - - - - - - - - - -

As they gathered on my kitchen-nook sofa to peer at the computer, thirteen-year-old Elena had one of her arms around the shoulder of handsome, fourteen-year-old Misha and placed the other on ten-year-old Anya's head. Her hand stroked Anya's hair, casually, affectionately.

I am referring here to another Anya—there seem to be many Anyas in Russia. The Anya I am writing about now is pretty but differently so than is the other. This one has straight, very dark, brown hair. A trace of Asian ancestry may be seen in her high cheekbones. Her eyes have a trace of an almond shape and are spaced wide apart. I wonder if in her that is diagnostic of Fetal Alcohol Syndrome rather than Far Eastern genes. I thought I noted FAS in the faces of a couple of other kids here but Anya, if she has it, does not show worrisome symptoms. For one thing, she does not seem deficient intellectually. Rather, she comes across as bright, certainly chatty. Yet ... and yet ... there is something else ... I noticed that hollow look on her face that is often seen in children who have been battered. Much can be seen in children's faces.

Children are lounging about—not in my kitchen, a welcome change, but in the large meeting room next door. It is a good scene. Some are chatting, most are hypnotized by television. The film they are watching, made for children in Soviet days, is about a Persian beauty and her hero boyfriend. Two younger boys, Vitalik and Zhenya, are sprawled on the floor, pushing wooden trains along imaginary tracks. The trains are among the few toys here.

Ten-year-old super Anya enters and plops herself down heavily. She has been crying for some reason. I ask her why. She shakes her head. "I don't want to talk about it," she says. I will never know. A vospitatilnitsa enters next, stands behind her, smoothes her hair and murmurs soothing words. I cannot understand them but the meaning is clear from the music of her voice.

Tears are impacted behind the eyes of several children, dammed up with nowhere to go. This is especially evident in Elena even when she is in a giddy mood, but Alicia is quite different. I can't imagine her crying— ever. She projects a sense of irrepressible joy, but it is of course possible that as I come to know her, I will need to revise this impression.

With a malicious grin, Zhenya makes a tight muscle in his upper right arm. He asks me to feel it. "Wow!" I say, "*Tyi ochen krepko!*" You are very strong. He punches me. We hand-wrestle. I grab him around the waist and toss him into the air. He squeals.

I leave the priut and take a stretch with the idea of going for a stroll. I desperately need exercise and fresh air. But once outside, it occurs to me that I miss the scene on the inside. I head back to the playroom, this time stopping in my room to grab my camera. When they spot it, the children line up individually and in groups and beg me to take their pictures. Some make silly faces but most act as if this were an important occasion. A few staff members pose with the children.

I finally take my walk. By now, I really need it. The children have not gone out today even though it is a bright Saturday, cold but invigorating. Why *didn't* they go out? It is not good for them to spend so much time inside. Like me, children require exercise, fresh air. Although Russians are preoccupied with health, many lead strikingly unhealthy lives, poor diet, no exercise, smoking and alcohol.

There are plenty of *vospitatilye* (plural of "child-care worker"), nurses and doctors around but there is no one to take the kids on a walk. Explain that to me!

I took my lunch at a table shared with little man Zhenya and two of his noisy buddies. After they finished, they quite properly bussed their dishes and marched out the door while wishing new arrivals a "*priatnivo appetita,*" good appetite. I continued my meal with two vospitatilye. We had borscht with sour cream, stewed meat of some kind along with mashed potatoes, a carrot salad and fruit compote for desert, plus cold tea. A fine meal. I thanked Irina, the cook, but apologized for not having finished the mashed potatoes.

"Next time we'll give you less," she said cheerfully.

- - - - - - - - - - - - - - - - -

One of the vospitatilye informed me that she has a daughter who is a forensic physician. "She must be very intelligent," I said. "Oh, yes, she is!" she said.

- - - - - - - - - - - - - - - - -

Every time I come up with a correct word or phrase, I am pleased with how much Russian I can handle but I still know far, far too little. I am frustrated, often feel stupid and lacking in dignity as well.

- - - - - - - - - - - - - - - - -

I tried to help wash the dishes. "You can*not*!" Irina the cook said firmly. "That is a job for the children. They get paid for it. Ten thousand rubles" (about two dollars).

- - - - - - - - - - - - - - - - -

It's now 3:30. Most of the kids are busy cleaning the dormitory, an activity called "*uborka.*" Everybody seems to be working hard. Furniture is pushed aside in a great flurry of activity, sweeping, mopping, dusting. Unfortunately, not everyone works with equal passion. Blond, bossy Anya is a prominent goof-off.

Anya arm wrestles me and makes giddy comments to one of the vospitatilye who is trying to find something useful for her to do.

Still, nobody has gone outside all day except me. I love taking walks. I think most children do, too. Normally, I learn, they do take walks. They are inside today because it is a Saturday, the occasion for the mother of all uborkas.

I therefore attempt to postpone the proposed walk. "Later," I explain. "After uborka." Sadly, my language skills are not up to communicating this thought. People look at me, bewildered.

Natalia Nikolaevna, the vospitatilnitsa in charge, probably thinks that my intent is to sabotage the work crew. She informs me that after everybody is done I may take them out. "First they must finish," she insists. "It is an important project."

"I know," I mumble in my best Russian.

- - - - - - - - - - - - - - - -

Alicia and the blond Anya, sister of Sasha, sneak off the work crew and show up in my kitchen nook. They attempt to convince me to let them play even more computer games. I remain steadfast. I tell them that they must go back to their uborka.

"Uborka is done," they say.

"Okay. That's nice. But I am busy now. You may watch me type, but no computer games."

After a few minutes, I say, "If uborka is done, then I am ready for a walk."

"With us?"

"Of course."

Just then Serogia and Misha, two of the big boys, wander into my room. They want to play games, too. They also want to quiz me about the American music group, Prodigy. It's no doubt famous but I never heard of it.

The guys borrow my cassette tape player. Loud rock music blares forth. Serogia explains that the music we are hearing is Prodigy, straight from America. "Do you like it?" he asks.

"*Normal'no*," I reply. So-so. I lie on the side of enthusiasm.

Throbbing pop music floods the room, first American and then Russian. The children sing and dance in their inimitable, zingy, fast-moving, unmistakably Slavic, style.

- - - - - - - - - - - - - - - -

It is four o'clock. The pale, orange sun can still be seen lowering toward the horizon. It will never fully retire because this is the season of St. Petersburg's famous White Nights. Who knows if there will be a walk for *any*body today? But uborka is finally over and done with. Kids drift back to my kitchen and busy themselves with computer games, their spirits high as ever.

- - - - - - - - - - - - - - - -

4:30 PM. We *did* take our long-awaited walk although it was not quite what I had in mind. Natalia Nikolaevna assigned the older Serogia to accompany me, me alone, just me. I had said something about a need to purchase toothpaste so she arranged for Serogia to help me with this utilitarian errand. But in fact all I wanted was to explore the neighborhood with a bunch of kids in tow. Motivated by mistaken kindness, Natalia Nikolaevna tried to spare me the pestering children. How was she to know that I had come all the way to Russia to be so pestered?

I tried to argue my case: "How about the *younger* kids? May I take a small group of them?"

"Perhaps next time," she said. "They have a lot more uborka to do just now."

Oh, no! The children had led me to believe that uborka was done with. Conned again. I had thought better of the little liars and was disappointed in myself for being gullible. I had envisioned a merry crew slipping and sliding along the frozen sidewalks, holding hands, perhaps a bit on the wild side yet convivial. Instead it was only Serogia and me.

But Serogia, as it turned out, was a fine fellow. I had no problems with him. It's just that he was one guy and there were sixteen others in my room at the time all of whom I want to know.

- - - - - - - - - - - - - - - - -

Serogia: He is fifteen, wiry, tough, laconic. I had noticed him with little kids coming across as bully but I've also seen him being rather sweet with his age-mates. Alone with me, he is silent and uncomfortable. He doesn't volunteer information and stammers awkwardly when he gives a one-word answer to a question I put to him. It's not just a matter of the language barrier. He knows a few words in English which he enjoys practicing and my Russian is bad but not *that* bad. When I asked, "What time do they serve supper at the priut?" he answered "Seven" in perfect English.

With considerable effort, I managed to coax even more information out of him. He told me that he had lived on the streets before coming to the priut. He allowed that Almus is a good place. I asked what he likes about it. "Everything," he said.

Then, surprise, he spontaneously came up with a few questions for me. An example: "Is there a lot of marijuana in America?"

Serogia lit a cigarette the moment we left the priut and, as we walked along together, he smoked it casually like a man of the world. We came to a small department store nearby—an "*Univermag*"—where I bought treats for the kids back at Almus. I handed Serogia a few candies in return for his services as guide. He mumbled something that I could not make out, very likely "*spasibo,*" thank you.

We returned about an hour later. The kids were still at work, scrubbing the floors and dusting the shelves. Uborka is no small thing.

- - - - - - - - - - - - - - - -

Surely there could be more happening on a beautiful winter Saturday than uborka! Why no outings, hobbies or clubs? It is admirable that the children are keeping their house in order but surely uborka brings that virtue to obsessive new heights!

- - - - - - - - - - - - - - - - -

An hour before dinner, a large group of kids crowded into my room again to play with the ever-popular computer. Although they drifted in and out, a consistent core remained throughout. This included Misha, Vitalik, Zhenya, the blond Anya, and the female Sasha[3] with an occasional guest appearance by Alicia. I kept things going by feeding cookies to them all, taking photographs[4] and allowing everyone a turn at fooling around with the cassette recorder and computer.

They employed the privilege creatively. Anya took the microphone. "This is the news," she announced. "Now we will interview some very important people. First we go to Alicia. What is your name? Do you like boys? Who is your boyfriend?"

The subsequent interviews followed much the same pattern.

It was a long, relatively calm session. Misha, at fourteen, was the most mature member of the group. He took possession of the computer for the greater part of the time while the younger children mostly watched. They respected his wishes. Just before dinner he allowed others their turns.

---

3   Certain Russian nicknames can refer to females or males. "Sasha" is one that comes to mind and "Zhenya" is another. "Pasha" is a third. There are probably others.

4   All of the photographs of Almus children, unedited and in color, may be seen on my Web site http://web.mac.com/ robertbelenky/

- - - - - - - - - - - - - - - -

The children all begged me to sit at their tables at supper. These were little, square tables, four places each. Good for conversation. I chose to join Sasha's and took a seat at her right. She was obviously pleased but, after gulping down a few bites food, scooted out of the dining room and did not return. Overwhelmed? Probably. The other three children chatted among themselves. About what? I have no idea.

One of the vospitatilye, a quiet, thoughtful woman whose name I could not keep in my head, took Sasha's place. We got into as complex a conversation as I've had so far in the Russian language. She was trained as an engineer, she said, but could not find work in her field. That's why she became a vospitatilnitsa. The job pays a meager sum—300,000 rubles a month, the equivalent of sixty US dollars. She supplements this with money from friends and from a daughter who teaches French and English in Finland. Things do not seem to be getting better for ordinary people in this country but she does not look back at the Communist days with anything like longing. She clings to the hope that the future will bring a better life.

I think that's a reasonably accurate translation.

- - - - - - - - - - - - - - - -

After dinner, a swarm of burbling children swarmed again into my sitting room to play computer games. As before, they were surprisingly polite. Hyperactive Zhenya was the first to arrive. He stuck his head in at the door and, grinning sheepishly, asked, "*Mozhno?*"—

may I? *"Konyechno,"* I said—of course. Eventually, I had about a dozen such guests. They hung out in my quarters for the longest time. It's now a little past ten. The last of them left only a moment ago.

- - - - - - - - - - - - - - - - -

Another surprise: There do not seem to be cliques among Almus residents comparable to what we know in America. This may be because children come and go so much in this particular institution. But, I am of the opinion that Russian children in general appear to tolerate or even to appreciate one another more than ours do. There are friendship groups but they appear to be fluid and I haven't seen anyone pointedly excluding or picking on anyone else. There is also some but, compared to America remarkably little, squabbling about such matters as: "My turn!" or "No fair!"

The four older kids, Serogia, Misha, Elena and Masha, tend to hang out together. And, there is a group of young girls that includes both Anyas, Alicia, Sasha, and Lyuba. Then there is the middle group of boys: the other Misha as well as Vitalik, Losha, the younger Serogia, and Artyom. Finally, there is the second male Zhenya, age only four, who floats from group to group as a sort of puppy dog but seems mostly to play with Vitalik who, although older—maybe eight—is on the immature side.

I first thought that the fourteen-year-old Misha and Lena were boyfriend and girlfriend but now I'm not so sure. Misha is a handsome, thoughtful, fourteen-year-old who often wears a pained expression and has eyes that are often reddened as if from crying. He likes to play chess on the computer. Lena, by contrast, is volatile and insecure although, like some of the others, tough in the manner of a street kid. She is given to hugging Misha, clinging to him tightly, and holding his hand. In this setting, it may well go no further than that although she definitely projects a touchy-feely aura bordering on carnality. On the other hand, she hugs most other people, girls as well as boys, her best friend, Masha, and various vospitatilye.

Misha and Lena have in common those oceans of tears dammed up somewhere behind their eyes that I have remarked on in others. It gives them a haunted look common among kids who lead hard lives. One sees the same look in Russia, Haiti, and the United States. It probably reflects histories of abuse. It is a scar of sadness.

The friendship groups may have been established before arrival in the priut. Almus is a neighborhood institution. Some relationships began in the community. Nonetheless, they seem more inclusive, more fluid and in some sense deeper than those I recall in America.

- - - - - - - - - - - - - - - - -

What do these kids need? What can I offer them? Personal affirmation is, I think, the way to go … if I can figure out how. It is not necessarily a matter of hugs—although in part it is. Words of encouragement may be more to the point. Probably to know the child should be the first step and in the process to give him or her the most positive feedback possible. I might tell them how beautiful they are. Corny. I can praise their accomplishments in drawing, writing, computer game-playing, sports, wit or kindness, and, despite our brand new relationship, comment on the degree, subtly conveyed, to which they are important to me. But I must mean everything I say or the gambit will fall flat on its face and make a bad job worse.

Mime comes into play here. Nonverbal communication. Handshakes, grins, punches, taking visible pleasure of their company.

I imagine that a focus on their value to me personally is the best way to go. I will reveal in being and action that I like them—if indeed I do. And *only* if I do. Fortunately, they are all quite likable ... so far and for the most part ... and so I do like them ... as a group and each person as an unique and remarkable individual.

Let us not minimize the centrality of animal needs such as eating and touching. Love-starved people engage in both. Caution: Make sure that neither becomes addictive.

Touching is a trickier matter than eating. But it can't, or shouldn't, be avoided. In most US public schools, hugging a child has been outlawed as tantamount to child abuse.

But perhaps *not* touching a needy child is also a form of child abuse. Children such as those who live in Almus *must* be touched—their hair must be brushed, they must be allowed to sit on one's lap and they must be embraced as the occasion warrants, with honesty, warmth, safety, and sensuality. Yes: Sensuality. But NOT sexuality. To work with any child, a person must know the difference not simply in terms of the law but in one's bones and from the depths of one's soul. We are talking here of something beyond instruction. It is consumed with mother's milk.

We should also be alert to the danger of infantilization. The reason to work with children is to facilitate maturation. A hug is a beginning, necessary to growing up but by itself insufficient. A child must come to stand on his or her own two feet, learn to work with others, and meet the challenges of the world together. Shielding children from such challenges is *per se* crippling.

Let us in these matters emulate our primate cousins who lovingly groom one another but do not confuse it with mating nor do they allow grooming to delay growing up.

- - - - - - - - - - - - - - - -

Dark haired Anya asked if I will be leaving the priut on Monday. "No," I said, "I will stay here for two weeks."

"Do you like Almus?"

"Yes," I said. Very much."

"Oh," she said. "Good."

- - - - - - - - - - - - - - - -

Dark-haired Anya spent much more time with Misha this evening than did Lena. The two of them hunched together over the computer for what seemed like hours. Anya has not quite hit puberty. Misha is in the full bloom of adolescence and I doubt that he had any romantic intentions toward Anya. From his point of view, she is a little kid. He is a sweet guy, a big brother.

I do not know what might be going through her mind.

- - - - - - - - - - - - - - - -

Sashinka ("little Sasha"), the other Anya's little sister who I thought to be sad, shy, and ambivalent about being close to adults, is surely all of that. But it is now clear that she can also be wild and aggressive albeit in a playful way. She just came careening into my room, yelling loudly and laughing uproariously about something that I could not begin to comprehend.

Her sister, Anya the Alpha, can be extremely boisterous, too. Much of the noise from both of them may have been put on for my entertainment.

Yet there is remarkably little acting out around here. Sure, this is a noisy bunch but they are mostly polite, well behaved, and appreciative of whatever is done for them.

- - - - - - - - - - - - - - - -

The kids, waiting for a turn on the computer, flipped through my Russian-English/English-Russian dictionary. They tried to help me improve my Russian vocabulary by finding words for me to memorize. Prepubescent Alicia picked out the word, "abortion." I pronounced it as well as I could but unfortunately did not have the linguistic skill to engage her in a discussion.

- - - - - - - - - - - - - - - -

"Goodnight, kids. Time for sleep," I said gently but firmly.

"*One* more game, Bob? Just *one* more game, please!"

"I'll give you *five* more minutes. But that's it."

Enter a vospitatilnitsa. She barked at the kids expertly,

economically, and effectively. Abandoning hope of the promised five minute reprieve, the children hopped off to bed without so much as a whimper. Russian women really know how to yell at kids. This marvelous lady was neither threatening nor insulting. Her manner was good-humored yet businesslike, a combination I can only dream of.

There is little evidence that children are routinely or excessively punished in any of the schools or programs I've visited in Russia so far, admittedly selected because they are known to be good. I have yet to see children kneeling in corners as they are made to do in Haiti nor have I heard of any who have been slapped, beaten, or made to work in penance for some transgression. They are simply asked to do what needs to be done. And, for the most part, they do it. Those who don't may be required to submit to a mild, symbolic chastisement, grounding in one's room for an hour or two. That's the end of it.

By contrast, we in the States tend to be obsessed with control schemes that we think to be scientific. Charts of reinforcement schedules, both negative and positive, are posted on the walls of our most up-to-date group homes. In Russia, a few well-honed words directed at a kid seems sufficient.

We have much to learn from Russian women.

- - - - - - - - - - - - - - - - -

There is a new crew of vospitatilye on duty today. All are nice enough but they constitute a different cast of characters than yesterday's who in turn were not the same as those of the day before. If I were a kid whose life lacked coherence, I would find it further disorienting to adjust to new caretakers daily.

Why can't each vospitatilnitsa be assigned to a particular kid at the time that he or she first enters the priut? The worker would continue in a mentoring role, advocate, counselor, or surrogate parent with that same child for as long as needed. Other people would wander on and off the stage—teachers, vospitatilye, police and relatives—but the person in the center would remain steadfast.

Is there a reason for the current arrangement? Maybe as the mother role gets diffused, the peer group becomes stronger to compensate. Peers by default then become the most salient source of support for the child.

Might that be why I notice so little arguing and fighting among these kids? Has the group become Mother?

- - - - - - - - - - - - - - - - -

High Culture: We took the Metro downtown to a museum to view an exhibition of Russian art work. Half the priut residents came along, eight kids. Only the newer ones expressed an interest in high culture. "The habitués are jaded," explained our trip leader, vospitatilnitsa Nadezhda Anatolevna, an articulate, well motivated woman. Her co-leader was Maria Vasilevna, likable, popular with the children but somewhat reticent. She assumed responsibility for little Zhenya rather than the entire group. She walked beside him, holding his hand.

We got off the train at the Gostinny Dvor station and

hiked a long way through the streets in central city. The children were in high spirits.

The girls held Nadezhda Anatolevna's hands and the boys grabbed mine. Although the girls wanted attention from me, too, and giggled when I gave it to them, none of them forced the hand issue uninvited. But the boys were otherwise. The fought over each of my hands. It was not just the relatively immature ones like Vitalik or the very young ones like Zhenya. It was all of them. Some who think themselves tough guys, Artyom and the younger Misha, not only held my hand but put their arms around me, hugging me awkwardly as we walked, nearly knocking me over.

Losha, a shy boy who has the look that comes from having cried a lot, said nothing when I took the initiative and offered my right hand to him. But he managed to hold onto it throughout the remainder of the trip leaving the other children to fight over my left one.

Sashinka trotted close by me, bumping me now and then as if by accident at which point she scooted away especially quickly if I offered her my hand or gave her even the smallest suggestion of attention.

Little Misha is a capitalist. He is into money—big time. He asked me for hard cash, any amount, any currency, at least a dozen times. I told him to get a job. "That's capitalism," I explained.

That kid has an ability to find cigarette butts wherever we go. I noticed him dive for one right outside the Gostiny Dvor Metro station. He collected them in a used Coca Cola paper cup. Then he and the two big boys, Losha and Artyom, lit up more or less publicly. The vospitatilye made no fuss nor did they even so much as acknowledge the misbehavior except for once toward the end of the trip when Nedezhda Anatolevna mildly confronted Misha. I do not know what she said but her manner was kindly and not confrontational.

A woman walking behind us on the Nevsky Prospekt lectured Misha on the dangers of smoking. She then turned on me and asked accusingly, "Why do you let these little boys smoke? Don't you know it's bad for their health!"

"Please, Madam," I said, "I'm a foreigner. I don't even speak Russian."

Another thing about Russians: Everyone considers him or her self to be responsible for everyone, particularly children. It is a charitable attitude ... but an annoying one.

We got to the exhibition a half hour before it opened. We decided to spend the intervening time wandering the city streets. We came to a small park by the River Neva. We took photographs of ourselves with a tame bear way in the background. We did not want to pay its manager to have the bear stand right beside us.

The children chased each other around a playground and climbed the famous statue of Peter the Great seated on his mighty steed. Nedezhda Anatolevna translated the sign for me. It read, "Do not play on the statue."

We returned to the museum, checked our coats and looked around. One could immediately tell that it was an interesting place for us grownups but probably a boring one for children, especially *our* children.

Mostly classical paintings were on exhibition along with a smattering of non traditional art and clothing design. Nobody, neither museum staff nor vospitatilye, attempted to explain anything to the kids. For their part, the kids did not race around with the wild abandon I feared but neither did they seem to gain much from the experience.

I treated everyone to ice cream afterwards. The kids said, "Spasibo, Dya-dya Bob," Thank you, Uncle Bob.

We had a late lunch back at Almus. Everyone was exhausted. Me, too. I took a much needed midday nap.

- - - - - - - - - - - - - - - - -

I hammered away on the computer in a futile effort to catch up on my notes.

Gradually it dawned on me that the priut was unnaturally quiet. I peered into the hallway. It was deserted. But I heard voices coming from the television room. So I opened the door. Three vospitatilye were in the process of organizing the children to form a priut "government." Kids were supposed to vote for one another to become "Minister" of Uborka or conflict resolution and this or that other position. One girl got to be minister of health, for example. Her responsibility was to see that the rooms were left in a tidy and healthy state each morning. Another was elected minister of culture. It was her job to organize next week's evening disco. Vospitatilnitsa Maria Vasilevna explained that this system was similar to that used by Russian Boy and Girl Scouts. It was a way of learning to be citizens in a democracy

The children were taking the whole thing quite seriously.

I noted that one vospitatilnitsa did not know the names of all the children. "Are you Anya or Sasha?" she asked.

- - - - - - - - - - - - - - - -

After the meeting, Nadezhda Anatolevna, Nadya, introduced me to her daughter, Anya, who is fifteen years old and has studied English since she was little. She is quite good at it. She competently translated a conversation between her mother and myself during which Nadya asked if, with Anya's help, I might be interested in gathering the children together, all of them at once, to answer whatever questions they might have about America or me.

"I would be delighted," I said.

Nadya ushered me back to the television/living room where the children sat politely waiting for us. They offered me a chair but I chose to sit on the floor, old hippy that I am.

Questions included, "Do you have a pet at home?" and, "Do you like Russian children?"

"Yes, a dog," to the first and a hearty, "Yes!" to the second.

I had questions for them: "Do they punish you here if you do something bad?" Sashinka waved her hand. When I called on her, she spoke briefly but with feeling.

Anya explained that Sasha didn't want to talk about punishment because she got so much of it at home.

"I'm not asking about what happens at *home*," I explained. "I want to know how you are treated in *Almus*!" Sasha seemed relieved but gave only a vague answer. Another child intruded to explain that physical punishment is definitely not part of the program here.

- - - - - - - - - - - - - - - - -

It is impossible to write anything at the moment because three boys, Artyom, the older Serogia, and Vitalik are staring at me as I type and asking rapid-fire questions that I can barely understand. I punch each of them on the arm in a comradely fashion.

- - - - - - - - - - - - - - - - -

I headed back to my kitchen salon with a gang of younger boys. A few other kids came along including the ever-present Sashinka, trailing the rest. I turned, roared at her like a fearsome lion, then grabbed her around the waist, tossed her over my shoulder and held her upside down by the ankles while galloping to catch up with the group. It was the proper treatment, I reasoned, for a shy, abused and neglected child. Sure enough, Sashinka giggled uncontrollably throughout and, for the first time in the three days of our acquaintance, did not simply run out the door but instead rushed *toward* me, relaxed and hilarious, demanding that I do it again. And again. And again.

- - - - - - - - - - - - - - - - -

"Perhaps," I asked Nadya's Anya, my teenage translator,

ignoring computer games for the moment, "while you are here, you could help me interview your mother. I have some questions I would like to ask her."

We ushered the children out of my kitchen office and, with Anya's help, Nadya—Nadezhda Anatolevna—and I conferred for about a half hour. Both of us wanted to explore the matter of punishment.

Nadezhda explained that misbehaviors are normally handled in Almus simply by talking with a child and helping him or her to understand that the misbehavior in question caused everyone to be disappointed in him or her. "We think better of you than that." If the transgression is very grave as, for example, involving drugs, the child may be asked to stay locked in his or her room for a few days, not talk with others and not participate in most activities. Meals, however, are exempt. Children are never made to miss meals here.

"Do *you* think it necessary to punish children?" she asked.

"Of course," I said, "but you need to know something about the child and his or her history to know what makes sense."

We talked about the kinds of trauma the children who come here are likely to have suffered. The litany was familiar: violence, beatings, sexual abuse, alcohol and drug involvement. Children like these are difficult to punish in a helpful way. Yet, like any young people, they require limits and the assurance that they are safe here, that adults know what they are doing, are motivated by love and are in control.

"In America," I offered. "We are principally concerned

with control, with punishments and rewards. In Almus people seem to know how to talk with children and to get the matter settled quickly and effectively. "But," I continued, "you sometimes ignore issues that we would consider important. I noticed, for example, that you didn't confront the boys who were smoking this morning on the trip to the museum."

"Well," Nadya replied. "These kids come from homes where everyone smokes. The children are addicted before they arrive. What can we do? If we forbid smoking, they'll do it anyway. So we have decided as a matter of policy just to let it go."

- - - - - - - - - - - - - - - - -

The weekly discotheque was going full blast in the basement. Everyone danced with everyone, big girls danced with any boys including little ones, big boys danced with whomever they could grab, and girls danced with girls. (But boys never danced with boys.)

Fast dances alternated with slow ones while colored lights swirled. The dance hall is the priut's gymnasium, decorated with streamers for the occasion. Artyom and Losha swung dangerously from ropes that hung from the ceiling. Everyone was in a great mood. The children put on a special show for me to demonstrate the steps they had been rehearsing.

- - - - - - - - - - - - - - - - -

I returned eventually to my office to work on these notes. But just as I settled in my chair, Serogia and Misha knocked. "*Mozhno—komputer, Bob? Nu?*

Pozhaaaliusta?" Bob, may I—the computer? Well? Pleeeze?

I invited them in "for a little while."

Now they are gone and I am headed to bed.

Morning. A hearty breakfast. I'm in my salon minding my own business. Three boys, Artyom, Sasha and Losha, watch me type. They hope that I will let them play computer games. Although I am getting sick of the whole thing, I just might. Blond Anya skips in and out. Little Misha does the same. For some reason none of these kids will be going to school today. Artyom said he has a sore throat but I cannot understand the excuses of the others.

Lena and Masha drop in on their way to school. "Bob! Give me three thousand rubles!" (about sixty cents) Lena, wearing a mischievous grin, demands.

"Why do you need three thousand rubles?"

"To buy chocolate," she said.

"Oh," I said. I reached into my dresser drawer and found some chocolate candy along with a handful of sweet cookies left over from yesterday's outing. I handed the stash to the girls. They scrambled out of the office, giggling.

At about five this morning I was dimly aware of my door creaking open and somebody sneaking into my room.

When I awoke a couple of hours later, I discovered that some of my sweets collection was gone. I had forgotten to lock the door last night. I don't know who the culprit was.

Morning. Tatiana Igor'ievna is still on duty. That's forty-eight hours, two shifts in a row, for her. After breakfast she attempted to get me into the local school for a visit. I had asked her how priut children function academically compared to other kids. "Let's ask the teachers," she suggested.

We walked out together into the dark, St. Petersburg winter morning. Oleg, a new younger boy, trotted along with us. It was a quarter past eight but the sun had not yet risen. It was cold, screeching-hard cold. Vospitatilnitsa Natalia Nikolaevna came, too, with her big, black dog, Tarzan, dancing by our side, leaping through the snow, running in circles and jumping clumsily onto her mistress.

The teacher announced that she did not have the authority to let me in. She suggested that we make a request to the school director. We did so and obtained his permission at once but then the original teacher on her *own* initiative declared the visit to be impossible after all. What could have gone through her mind? Maybe she thought I was there to evaluate her. I tried unsuccessfully to assure her that my interest was entirely with the children.

I observed from the corridor. As Tatiana Igor'ievna talked with his teacher, Oleg sat awkwardly, alone in the classroom, while children chased each other merrily up and down and every which way.

Most came to school accompanied by their mother or

father. Parents helped them remove their heavy winter coats and hang them properly on hooks. The local kids were well dressed compared with the priut residents. Some brought skis. (Did they ski to school along the housing project walkways or was this for after school?) This is hardly an affluent neighborhood but generally children seem well cared for. Oleg, our ragged urchin, stood out like a sore thumb in this crowd.

Tarzan bounded into the classroom. Then out again and in again at his pleasure but I, a human being, was denied entry. Is there no justice?

- - - - - - - - - - - - - - - -

The next morning, Anya and her sister, Alicia, asked me to walk them to school and sit in on their class. I told them that yesterday I had tried to do just that with Oleg but was prevented by the teacher. Alicia said that today a different teacher will be in charge.

"Try again," she said.

I did. Alicia arranged the visit with no difficulty. The teacher, Galina Viktorovna, welcomed me. After class she took me aside to fill me in on Alicia and her needs. Unfortunately, I managed to understand only some of what she said.

"Alicia misses her mother and her work, which she is well able to do, suffers as a result." She went on to explain something about Alicia's mother but I could not follow her.

Alicia is in the "second class" which apparently does not correspond to our second grade. "Second" as she used it must mean "remedial." The children range in age from six or seven to eleven, Alicia's age. There are a total of twenty-five students. Although Alicia was one of the oldest, there were several not much younger.

Kids run to meet me. Alicia makes introductions. She has many friends. The class begins with stretching exercises. Galina Viktorovna is young, pretty, and comfortably in charge. The children obviously take to her. The classroom is arranged formally by US standards. unmovable tables, two students per table, tables lined up in two rows.

Alicia sits in the very rear on the left. What is the significance of that placement? Is she among the slowest? The fastest? Is she more in need of help than others? Or less?

The class proceeds in a question-and-answer format. There is considerable use of the blackboard. Children take turns writing on it.

Alicia is not paying attention. Others are busy writing in their notebooks. But she simply sits, staring off into space. Gradually, she starts to write but vaguely as if in a dream. When she is called upon for a turn at the board, she performs reasonably well.

Two minute break for more stretching exercises.

Later: Alicia half-raises her hand, waves it lazily, but is not called on. Goes back into her dream state. Puts her head on her folded arms as if to sleep but jerks herself into a nominally alert position after a few minutes.

Again she raises her hand ambivalently but again is not called on.

The class continues for forty-five minutes. Several

children become restless but most remain remarkably attentive. My own attention is failing. ...

Class dismissed.

- - - - - - - - - - - - - - - -

I am back in Almus observing four children in a tutorial class. Beyond attendance at the local school, they are tutored five times a week in the priut to help them catch up to grade level. They include two little guys, Oleg and Andrusha, and two girls, the dark haired Anya and her sister, Alicia.

The tutor, Klavdia Aleksandrovna, a person of considerable experience, is moonlighting from her full-time teaching job elsewhere. She welcomes me. I decide to focus on the two girls since they hang around me more. I know them better than I know the boys.

Anya is restless, unable to focus. Manipulative. Asks Klavdia Aleksandrovna to check her work. Klavdia Aleksandrovna rotates among the four children, spends a few minutes with each. Her approach is low-key, gentle but businesslike. Oriented to task.

Alicia sticks to her work without looking at Klavdia Aleksandrovna.

Klavdia Aleksandrovna strokes and brushes Anya's hair with both hands as she talks with her. Makes a pony tail. Searches for something to tie it with.

The lesson is from a textbook. Anya makes a big show of being bored. She yawns, stretches and wiggles in her seat.

The task is simple math. Anya's work habits are chaotic. But, Alicia is relatively focused.

Anya has slight strabismus, a wandering eye. I wonder how it affects her vision and thus her ability to work. Several children here have that problem.

Klavdia Aleksandrovna is old-fashioned in looks and manner. She is middle aged and patient, indeed grandmotherly. She often purrs, "khorosho" (good) and "molodiets" (good kid).

Alicia is moody rather than merely inattentive. At the moment she appears depressed, Her head rests on her folded arms. Perhaps she is tired. I have seen her become quite animated on other occasions but never tired, and never out of control.

Anya, with a manipulative grin, calls again for Klavdia Aleksandra's attention. She whimpers in an exaggerated baby voice, looks to me for affirmation and grins cunningly. She tries to entice me to respond, but I remain stedfast. I wave her off dismissively.

Klavdia Aleksandrovna becomes visibly irritated with Anya but controls herself while maintaining a sharp eye on her.

Anya sits with one hand on her cheek, the other over her shoulder and twisted somehow behind her back. She stares blankly ahead. Then she peers at me again and makes a silly face. I don't respond.

The class goes on in much the same way for forty-five minutes. I take my leave toward the end. This is a very long time for someone with Anya's attention span. She feels stupid. In my opinion, remediation with someone like Anya must consist of leading her into repeated success experiences. Long lessons, even good ones such as this, generate exhaustion, failure and a wretched sense of self.

- - - - - - - - - - - - - - - -

Natalia Nikolaevna was one of three people on duty today. A dedicated woman in her forties, highly cultured, she wears wire-frame glasses and a long skirt. She looks like someone out of a nineteenth century photograph. She is almost nunlike in appearance, ("A *nun? Me?*" she later exclaimed as she read a translation of these notes. "You don't know what you are *talking about!*") but has a fanciful, irreverent streak. She is invariably interesting, always serious yet oddball, formal yet bohemian, structured yet fun-loving. An intellectual, she makes continual, occasionally successful, efforts to interest her motley crew of children in Russian high culture by which she means visits to museums, theaters, concerts, exhibitions, and monuments. It is unlikely fare for urchins, I thought, but how brave of her to make the attempt.

- - - - - - - - - - - - - - - -

Not much was going on so I told Natalia Nikolaevna that I was heading off to the photo store to get my latest films developed and printed. Perhaps, I suggested, some of the children might want to come with me. She rounded up four volunteers and announced that she herself would join us. The kids included Alpha Anya, Andrei, macho Zhenya, and fourteen-year-old Lena who, I had been informed, was grounded because of "bad behavior." Someone relented. Most likely Natalia Nikolaevna.

Natalia Nikolaevna took us by bus to the Lomonosovskaya Metro station. Nearby was a one-hour Kodak picture processing shop. We left off the film and took the Metro to the Gostiny Dvor station and walked from there a few blocks to Voskreseniya Khristova—Christ's Resurrection—Church, a soaring example of nineteenth-century sacred architecture, recently reconstructed. It is adorned with onion domes and inlaid mosaic icons on the inside walls. Although perhaps an unlikely place to bring them, our kids were at least polite if not fully pleased to be there.

Was this a typical destination for Almus field trips or was it chosen to impress me? I could not say.

Skipping along the street, Lena stopped a respectable gentleman to bum a cigarette. Natalia Nikolaevna said nothing. In my pitiful Russian I mumbled something to Lena about how smoking could ruin her health. She pretended to ignore me but I suspect that she caught the message.

We walked through the park near the Russian State Museum, the Mayakovsky Gardens, and back again to the Metro through "Passage," an upscale mall. The children loved racing through it.

- - - - - - - - - - - - - - - -

The photos came out well. The children were pleased and helped me distribute them. Each child for whom there was an individual portrait was given a copy to keep and we made an exhibition on the wall of all the group pictures. I announced that these were now the collective property of Almus. I used the word "collective" on purpose. There seems to be a big thing in this country about the word "collective."

- - - - - - - - - - - - - - - -

My kitchen nook is filled again with sweet children with their noses in computer games. A knock on the door. Enter Valeria, the young, professional translator that Jeff, the director of the US branch of Vrachi Mira, had promised to send to help me interview children. Valeria is short, thin, young and hip. She has spent time in the States as a student and speaks rapidly in almost accentless English. I am sure the kids will go for her immediately.

Serogia-the-elder volunteered to be our first interviewee. Serogia, the guy who accompanied me to the store the other day, had lived in the streets since the age of seven. He is friendly, canny, and possibly bright but in my attempt to speak with him in my Chico-Marx-Russian, I had found him to be inarticulate. Of course, I was the linguistically challenged one. Now, with Valeria on board, I would be able to understand him. Who knows? He might prove articulate.[5]

I am Sergei. You may call me Serogia. I am fourteen. My favorite age is two. I was living with my family when I was two.

My life has been very long. I didn't grow up in a family. I grew up on the streets, near flowers. I mean near kiosks where flowers were sold. I was seven when I left

---

5   See the appendix for our interview schedule.

my family. How did I survive? I begged for money. I did what I could.

The reason I left my family was that I didn't want to go to school. I wanted freedom. So I lived in the streets until I was twelve or thirteen. Nobody took care of me, no adults and no older kids. Nobody takes care of anybody in this world. Everybody is out for himself.

I liked living on the streets. I often hung out at a hotel to help foreign people. I got things from them. I slept in attics and deserted buildings and hotels. There were problems of course. The police bothered us and even beat us up. When I lived in the airport, they caught us. They liked to catch us around seven in the evening and keep us at the station until maybe eight in the morning and beat us up all night and make us do different things to humiliate us.

You want examples? Well, they made us do physical exercises until we were half dead. I've heard about sexual abuse but they never did any of that kind of stuff to me.

How did I get to Almus? Well, there was this other shelter called Sinaya Vorona (Blue Crow). I was taken there by the police. Then that shelter got closed down and so I tried to live with my family again, my mother, my sister, and my mother's boyfriend, but I kept running away because my mother's boyfriend used to beat me up real bad.

I was caught by a policeman and was sent to another shelter, Vera (Truth), and then I got sent here. I don't know why they picked this place.

I don't know what I want my life to look like in twenty

years. I guess I would want to be alive. I might die. Who knows? If I live, I might have a family. I don't know what kind of work I would want to do. I don't think about my future.

When I die, my friends will say, "He died and that's good."

If I marry, I will have children because everyone likes to have children. If I had a good job and earned a lot, I would want to have eight. I like children.

If the whole world were listening, I would say, "Dear People of St. Petersburg, Be Happy! Have lots of children!"

I think I will be a good father. My own father is very strict but maybe also just a little bit kind and caring. I would take care of my family and my children. I would hit my kids only if they deserved it. I wouldn't be a drunk. I think I'd be like my mother who drinks on holidays but that's all. And then she only takes maybe two shots.

My father drinks but not too much. He works a lot and I don't see him. He's not living with my mother.

The reason I left home was that everybody was finding fault with me. They wouldn't let me do things. When I have kids, I won't keep them from doing things.

I like it here at Almus—a lot. But there's one thing I don't like: The vospitatilye don't do enough for the kids. Yesterday, for example, I had problems with my stomach. I had diarrhea and had to get to the bathroom but they wouldn't let me. They made me stay in my room.

If I have complaints like that, there's nobody here I can talk to about them.

I found it noteworthy that this child of the streets longs for the time that he was a baby and living with his family, presumably cared for. Of equal note is his imagining a future with a family of his own. Although short on specifics, he believes that he will be a good father. I wonder about such visions. Do they help heal? Are they ever realized? What would it take to make such dreams come true?

- - - - - - - - - - - - - - - - -

Anya, the one I have seen as an in-charge sort of person:

You may call me Anya. I am eleven. I would rather be fifteen because a fifteen-year-old can go out until one in the morning. I would like to hang out with my friends until then. We wouldn't do much, nothing bad, just walk around.

I don't have many friends. I am always sad. I am never happy. If I tried to explain why, I couldn't. I would cry.

When I look in the mirror, what do I see? I see a very ugly girl. I don't go to school now because I am not from this neighborhood. I don't have the papers. I used to like school but I never did well. The only thing I liked about school was the holidays.

Okay. If you really want to know, I am sad because my grandmother died. It was during an operation. I didn't go to the funeral but I saw her body at the morgue.

I was surprised by what Anya said and the depressed tone with which she said it. In the priut and on our trip to town this morning, she has been a lively kid, full of fun and mischief, an active leader as well as a cheerful pest. But during the interview, she pulled into herself. She seemed a different person.

- - - - - - - - - - - - - - - -

Sasha, Anya's Sister:

My name is Alexandra. I like to be called Sasha. I don't mind if you call me Sashinka. I am ten years old. My sister, Anya, is a year older than me. We really like each other. I like this priut but this is the only one I like. I first was sent to Vera. In Vera the vospitatilye were real mean. The ones here are very good. The ones at Vera don't care about kids.

When I first came here I was scared. I didn't like it at all but now I do. I'm here because my mother died. A car ran over her. That was less than a year ago. We tried living with our father after that. But once Anya and I went to the neighbors house because our father was hardly ever home. When our father came back and Anya knocked at the door, he said something to her. I don't know exactly what it was but I know he used very bad words. After that, we got our coats and left. We just walked out the door. We were in a store when the police caught us and we were sent to Priut Vera.

Sometimes when he is drunk, my father likes me. When he doesn't drink, he doesn't like me. Sometimes he beats me after drinking. When he beats me, he beats me very hard. Sometimes I cry. Sometimes I hide. But my mother never beat us. She loved us.

I have no other relatives. I loved my mother. My grandmother also died not so long ago. I loved her even more than my mother.

I like to draw but I'm not very good at it. I want to be an artist when I grow up.

The story—or is it the myth?—of the parent who is kind only when drunk is one I have heard before. It must be a comforting formulation. Interesting that Sasha, the overtly more withdrawn sister, is able to talk about so much that Anya, the more dominant of the two, could not. Why didn't Anya mention the death of their mother? I don't know the answer to any of these questions. I don't know anything. These questions deserve to be highlighted even if the truth behind them is never revealed. This is not a didactic lesson.

- - - - - - - - - - - - - - - - -

At breakfast, dark-haired, eleven-year-old Anya - not the one I just wrote about - said, "Bob! Eat your *kasha* (cereal). It is good! Why don't you *eat?*"

"Who are you," I said. "My *mother?*"

- - - - - - - - - - - - - - - - -

Blond Anya took over my computer for most of the afternoon. There were others in my room, most of them boys. They did not challenge Anya's dominance but instead passively observed her play. At one point, however, Vitalik, visibly intimidated, whispered to me that he would like a turn. I advocated for him. Anya offered him her chair with no fuss but a few minutes later there she was back in her old place in full command of the computer. Vitalik had deferred to her.

Her timid sister Sashinka by contrast gives an occasional

boy a whack on the head if she doesn't like where he sits, what he does or what he says.

The boys in this priut, who may or may not be typical of Russian males, tend to be gentle. Some of them, Vitalik for example, are also immature socially. Others, like big Serogia, walk with a swagger and look as if they are in charge of everything and everyone while in fact they may also be passive and carry as little weight with the Alpha Girls as the sweet ones.

Most of these guys—at least the preadolescents among them—are easy to hug. No need to roughhouse. Just put an arm around them and they melt.

Generally, the girls in Almus seem a tougher and noisier lot than girls I am used to in the States. But ten or so years from now, they will probably be beaten by sweet boys much like these fellows here.

- - - - - - - - - - - - - - - - -

Fifteen-year-old Anya, competent in the English language, daughter of vospitatilnitsa Nadya, knocked on my door to ask if I needed her.

"Let's interview more kids!" I said.

- - - - - - - - - - - - - - - - -

We began with Alicia, 10, sister of the dark-haired Anya.

How did I get to live in a priut? My mother was put in prison because she has a bad drinking problem and broke a wall. I don't get to see her any more. I have one brother, Denis. He's eight and lives with my father.

And I have a sister, Anya, who is here in the priut with me. You know Anya.

My father and mother are divorced. He has a new wife. He doesn't drink or smoke. I like my father and get to see him most Saturdays. I also like his new wife. I have problems with my mother though. She sometimes left us alone in the house and locked the door so we couldn't get out. My mother will be in prison for a long time, I think. I worry about her.

I like it very much in Almus. I like the clothes they give us. And I like all the vospitatilye. And I really like school. But I want to go home.

- - - - - - - - - - - - - - - - -

Anya, 11, Alicia's sister

I like it here okay. What happened is that mama got put in prison. But it wasn't her fault. It was her second husband's. She has had three husbands. My father was her first. Anyway, my mom and her husband stole electricity from the city which they sold to buy clothes and food for us kids. They got caught by the neighbors who called the police.

Mom had a bad drinking problem. One night at three o'clock she was very drunk and went after us with a knife. She told us to call our father and we did and we went to his place for the next couple of days.

My stepfather doesn't do anything around the house. He made us haul water and do the cleaning and everything. He drinks and used to beat mama. He beat us, too.

I like to spend time with my father. He takes us out.

I don't think about my mother a lot but sometimes I have nightmares about her. I dreamed that somebody was killing her with a knife.

This priut is only so-so. It's okay in some ways but I want to go home. I don't like any of the boys because they fight all the time. The vospitatilye are so-so, too. Some are nasty.

I like school, though. I don't do very well but I want to be a teacher when I grow up.

- - - - - - - - - - - - - - - -

Vitalik, 9

I don't have an otchestvo (a middle name derived from the first name of the father; a patronymic) because I never knew my father or anything about him. I don't remember anything about my life.

I came here from another priut. The name of it is Vera. I was brought there by my mother.

I don't know if I have brothers or sisters.

My mother used to call me very bad words and beat me. She beat me once when we came back home after going for a walk because I was too dirty.

I like this priut because they let me be sick here. My mother made me go for walks even when I was sick.

I miss my mother only a little. She comes to visit me sometimes on Mondays.

- - - - - - - - - - - - - - - -

Masha, 13, an innocent-looking girl who has spent much time on the streets.

I don't want to live at home. That's why I'm here. I can't stand home because my mother drinks so much. She forgets everything when she gets drunk. Like she looks for cigarettes and when she doesn't find them, she says I stole them. She blames me for everything. When my mother drinks a lot, she also smokes a lot. I want to get away from her but she doesn't like it when I do. She locks me up in my room. One day I just left and got sent to this priut.

Life is interesting here. You want to know what is interesting? Everything!

The only problem I have here is that big Serogia hits me. But I hit him back.

I don't like school. I don't like either the kids or the teachers. I am in seventh grade. When I was younger, I was a good student. Then I started cutting school and lying, telling people that I was on my way to school. But I would go to the Metro instead or to my friends' houses.

Someday I want to have a good job, a good husband, a good apartment, and lots of children. Well, only two children; maybe that's enough. I want to be a doctor, a doctor who works with children. I decided just now that I better start going to school and do well if I'm going to be a doctor.

My hobbies are sports, disco dancing and batik. I love aerobics. And tennis.

My father left me when I was four. I never see him

but I love him. Now I have a step father who hits me sometimes. I think a lot about my real father and keep photographs of him.

- - - - - - - - - - - - - - - -

Mikhail, 14

You may call me Misha.

I was taken here by a policeman. I had bad problems with my father. He drinks and he beats me. A lot. A whole lot. I ran away from home and lived with friends of the family. I was taken here on April 15, 1997. I don't want to go home ever again.

My mother left the family when I was three. She took my sister and my father took me. I didn't like that.

(Long silence.) I don't want to talk about it. (His eyes redden.)

- - - - - - - - - - - - - - - -

Early evening. I come upon two of the vospitatilye who were at work on a crafts project with a small group of children. They are making beautiful wall decorations together out of birch bark, moss, dried flowers and berries.

- - - - - - - - - - - - - - - -

Three boys were punished tonight. They were made to stand for about ten minutes in the common room while other kids dutifully ignored them. I have no idea what they did to deserve this but I was told that the penalty was chosen democratically by the children's governance assembly.

- - - - - - - - - - - - - - - -

There is only one man on this evening's shift, Alexander Viktorovich, a.k.a. Sasha. He is a *vospitatel,* a male childcare worker.

I can't figure him out.

Sasha is thin, tense and has blond hair and a trimmed mustache. He dresses neatly, almost too neatly. He stays mostly in the background and sometimes has a look of exasperation on his face. Is he withdrawn? Inaccessible? Yet the kids seem drawn to him. Odd. It is safe to say that he is very intelligent. A little while ago Alicia called him "dya-dya Sasha," Uncle Sasha, a term of obvious endearment. But he seems to offer little of himself.

I can't figure him out.

I write this at a few minutes past eleven at night. I need a glass of tea and a slice of the good, Vermont cheddar cheese that I contributed to the staff kitchen. Who should be there just as I was writing about him? Sasha! He was busy tutoring the younger Serogia in math. At this late hour? Impressive.

Sasha greeted me. I remarked on his dedication. He nodded a vague "spacibo." Serogia certainly needs attention, a great deal of it I would say, particularly from a gentle man. But after eleven at night?

I think I have Sasha figured out. He is a gentle man.

- - - - - - - - - - - - - - - -

Sasha and I run into each other again at breakfast. We sit at the same table. "Serogia is an interesting boy," I venture. "Yes," says Sasha. "Very neurotic but very bright. Interesting, certainly, particularly to a psychologist like yourself."

"He longs for a family," say I.

"Who doesn't?" says he.

- - - - - - - - - - - - - - - - -

Kids working quietly on their own projects transform my office into a homey place, a club house. The spirit possesses me and I hand out candy without being asked.

With ample art supplies, there is less energy directed to me personally. There was almost no sitting on my lap this morning—except for little Zhenya and he lasted no more than a few minutes. The scene today is distinctly task-oriented.

One the other hand, one might think that things have deteriorated. A few days ago the kids didn't argue about whose turn it was on the computer but now they do. It depends on how you look at it. The neat thing is that they are able quickly to work it out. After only a brief chorus of, "Me first! Me second! Me third," they manage to agree on an order and pretty much stick to it. Each turn was to last exactly five minutes. I was asked to keep track. I did so, as fairly and efficiently as I could.

Although blond Anya is surely strong willed, when her turn on the computer ends she manages to step back for the next kid. But then she hovers over that person's work, telling him (the masculine pronoun is used here because most of the time the only people here for this incident were several boys - plus Anya) what to do and grabbing the mouse to demonstrate.

Anya's sister, Sashinka, wanders in and out of the room. Her character is just as strong as Anya's but she shows little or no motivation for leadership. Her contribution is limited to smacking an occasional boy on the head.

Other neat kids drop in for a visit, again mostly boys. The younger Misha for example. He's the guy who collects dirty cigarette butts on the street. He is given to making obscene jokes and pushing people around. There is also the male Sasha who sneaks a cigarette when he can. And then, of course, we have the big Serogia, the Central Castings street kid.

These big guys are strong. And tough. They take pleasure in wrestling.

But the aggressive girls—Anya, Sasha, and fourteen-year-old Lena, the one who bummed a cigarette from a gentleman on the street—seem to enjoy rough physical contact, wrestling, punching, chasing, pinching, as much as do the boys. Their manner, though combative, is in its own way conventionally feminine in that with them aggression is combined with theatrical cuteness.

These Russian kids as a whole come across to me as lively, uncool, eager to please and capable of expressing all sorts of fresh and positive emotions from appreciation to enthusiasm to actual love. I think American kids are cooler, at least on the surface.

Russian kids are products of a far more communal culture than we have experienced. This may be related to the Communist legacy but more likely it antedates that regime by millennia. Elements of that culture may also been seen in Russian Orthodox churches where instead of sitting in pews that face a single alter, people wander in small groups from icon to icon. The priest follows. It is the group that is central, not the altar. One sees reminders everywhere here of that ancient, still vital, culture.

These are but impressions, generalizations, speculations. But one cannot visit Russia for long without becoming aware of the dynamic tension between community and the personal, *obschinost,* on the one hand and *lichnost* on the other. Historically, the tension has been resolved in favor of community at considerable cost to the personal.

The sense of community is palpable in this shelter although times are changing. The lure of America despite its well-known anomie is seductive. A wave of the personal is rising in Russia and threatening to destroy everything communal in its path, the good and the bad alike, from generosity to social responsibility to collective labor to pious charity and to the horrors of the GULAG.

- - - - - - - - - - - - - - - - -

It is extremely cold tonight. They say it will reach thirty-five below Celsius. At forty below, Celsius and Fahrenheit read the same. It was frigid in my room so I went downstairs to ask the concierge if he could find me an extra blanket. He directed me to a door at the end of the hall. "They'll give you what you need in there," he said.

The door opened on a new continent, a shining white infirmary complete with a uniformed nurse whom I had met several times before but I had never taken the time to inquire about her role.

I knew nothing of the isolation ward. Someone might have mentioned it to me about it but because of my fragile command of the Russian language, what they said must have escaped me.

Four kids were gabbing together, a six-year-old boy, two thirteen-year-olds—a boy and a girl—and a fifteen-year-old boy. There was to be a fifth child, a girl who had returned to her family for a few days and was due back momentarily. These kids were all new to the priut and as such needed to be quarantined for ten days while medical tests were run on them and whatever contagious diseases they may have brought from the streets can be treated or at least identified and contained.

Meanwhile, they have nothing to do but hang out and wait for the results of the tests.

"Bored?" I asked.

"No way!" the thirteen-year-old boy said, giving the nurse, a young, pretty, maternal-looking woman, a big hug.

As we talked, Lena and Masha from the upstairs program ran in. They knew a couple of the new kids from around the neighborhood and immediately engaged them in an animated discussion. (Is such contact permitted in a proper quarantine?)

- - - - - - - - - - - - - - - - -

Life is not at all bad in Almus. It is far more stimulating than in your average two-parent family. It is more like summer camp with a touch of familial spirit. However, thanks to the fact that Saturday has rolled around again and uborka is on the docket, today is likely to be a bit on the dull side except for the disco that is scheduled for tonight. But tomorrow all who those interested may go to a museum or the theater.

I asked the older Misha, "Do you like it here?"

"I *love* it," he said with conviction.

"How does it compare to living with your family?"

"*Much* better."

Yet each day there is that infernal staff rotation that strikes me—but apparently no one else—as a major lapse in program design.

- - - - - - - - - - - - - - - - -

The new shift has arrived! The vospitatilye are surrounded at once by chirping children who embrace them and are petted by them. Blond Anya—"Alpha Anya" in my notes—breathlessly tells Tatiana Urovna that she visited the dentist yesterday and got *four* fillings!

Tatiana Urovna says, "Oh wow! Open your mouth and let me *see!*"

Anya opens her mouth wider than one would have thought possible. Tatiana Urovna peers in, charmed. "Beautiful," she says.

Tatiana Urovna has her own family, two boys. She

showed me their pictures and later when they visited here the other day, I met them. While at work, she probably thinks about them. Does she think about Anya when she is at home?

Is it really essential, I wonder, for every child to be at the center of a particular grownup's life?

Pleasant though Almus may be, it is not home. Replete with surrogate parents, actual parents are absent. No child is at the center of any grownup's life. Speaking for myself, I feel love for these children. But when I return home, their images will slip from my mind and I will think about my grandchildren a whole lot more.

Okay. Almus may not be a surrogate family but maybe it is good mental health .... Abused and neglected children chasing each other, laughing, being treated in an honest, respectful, good-humored manner; eating well, properly housed, clothed, educated, not beaten; protected from harm, safe from drunks. How much more does life offer any of us?

Yet problems remain. Almus, like all *priutye* (plural of priut), humane and otherwise, while successful to a large extent with younger children, cannot address the myriad developmental, intellectual and idealistic needs of adolescents. Something more is required for the older children, something designed specifically for their age group, discussions perhaps, challenge activities; specific preparation for living in a country where economic opportunities for young people are sorely limited.

But Almus is at least a good start. There is much here to build on.

- - - - - - - - - - - - - - - -

Four vospitatilye are on duty at once during daytime hours and two at night. The day staff also includes a cook and a nurse. There are three shifts. Each lasts twenty-four hours for the two night people, twelve hours for the other two. Night work is alternated so that a day shift does not follow a long night.

It is an awkward arrangement if not for the staff then certainly for the kids. It means that every day there is a whole new team on duty that does not return again for another three days. Children are constantly obliged to adjust to new personalities and approaches. And staff work to the point of exhaustion, absenting themselves from their own families every three days. Program development and continuity are thereby crippled and, worse, the probability that a child will become attached to any of these potential parent surrogates is slight.

With a staff of twelve, surely better arrangements could be invented. Might there not, for example, be a day staff and a separate night staff, both to be supplemented by relief teams on weekends? This would not be a perfect solution but might be an improvement.

- - - - - - - - - - - - - - - -

I was told later that, while everyone dislikes the current staffing arrangement, it cannot be changed. The reasons are bureaucratic and at a governmental level. It has to do with legislated salary schedules. I have no idea what is involved. There is no choice. It must be tolerated.

Yet, despite everything, vospitatilye work hard and

remain pleasant. They are smart, strong and devoted to the children.

And they love their tea breaks. As do I.

- - - - - - - - - - - - - - - -

Life in Russia is not easy. One of the four vospitatilye bearing the name, Tatiana, this one a particularly sensitive, cultured and hardworking person, explained this morning that she and her husband both have full-time jobs, she as vospitatilnitsa and he as skilled construction worker. She described him as "a worker who is also an intellectual." They read together and classical music is important in the life of their family. They are both university trained. They have two children. Yet, despite impressive backgrounds and character, they cannot earn enough money to survive. They must supplement their salaries with monthly contributions from her mother's meager pension.

- - - - - - - - - - - - - - - -

"Alla Pavlovna," I said to Vrachi Mira's Director of Medicine, "I cannot understand the vospitatilye. They are well educated, intelligent, vibrant, excellent with the children, and they work long hours for virtually no money. Yet they maintain an attitude which under the circumstances can only be described as bizarrely cheerful. How is that to be explained?"

"It's an old Communist attitude," she answered. "All those people who work at Almus are of my generation, middle aged. No young person today would work like that. Under the Communists, you worked because you believed that the work was important. You were idealistic.

You didn't do it for money. You didn't do it for your self. You did it for society. You would be embarrassed to so much as mention monetary concerns.

"You see, the reality of our society is complicated. It's not what you read in the papers. The Communists were certainly awful and many of us, including myself, despised them. But there was much about our way of life then that was moral in an almost religious sense. The Communist line on working for the community rather than for personal profit was not unlike the Russian Orthodox Church's belief in selfless charity. One cannot view life through a single lens."

- - - - - - - - - - - - - - - - -

"Alpha Anya," has become one of my favorite kids but I do not show it and remain absolutely even handed. She has been assigned to mop my room this week as part of her uborka. She is going about it professionally. She rightly considers this job to be an honor. But I find it a bit of a stretch to see her as cleaning woman rather than a wise kid who is seizing an opportunity for personal time on the computer.

Soon Alicia, another fine kid, joins Anya and together they become my work crew. They are actually working hard, giggling as they go. I hand out generous gifts. Cookies.

- - - - - - - - - - - - - - - -

Dr. Alla Pavlovna and I met this afternoon in her downtown office. Jeff Groton, the director of the St. Petersburg branch of New York—based Doctors of the World, participated and translated. We discussed

Almus, went over some thoughts about community mental health, "social medicine" as they call it here.

"Almus is the best priut we have in this city," Alla Pavlovna explained. "It is of such high quality because of Makarich, its director and founder. You have not yet had a chance to meet him but eventually you will. He understands children and the importance of a homelike atmosphere. He went out of his way to hire the very best people as vospitatilye. He found intelligent, cultured women—and me!—to work with him. Each of us has something of value to offer children. The vospitatilye take kids on educational excursions all the time to the theater, to museums, to art shows. Children of the sort we deal with would normally never be exposed to such influences.

"The program, beyond being educationally rich, is also multifaceted. Did you know that in addition to the fifteen or so children who live in the priut itself, there are another forty or more in affiliated foster care?"

We moved on to the topic of social medicine—community mental health—which interests Alla considerably although she claims not to know much about it. "The French office of Vrachi Mira, *Médecins du Monde,* also based in this city," she explained, "has been practicing it successfully for some time. Although the American office is limiting its efforts to conventional medicine, everyone agrees that to work with the Almus population, there must be some form of outreach. That means getting to know the children in the community and gaining their confidence as well as that of their parents."

With respect to community involvement, Alla Pavlovna

is proud of all the priutye affiliated with Doctors of the World—especially Almus. Unlike a *dietskiy dom*—an orphanage—or an internat—a boarding school, a priut is a seamless part of its community. It serves as a respite for parents, a source of mentoring for them, and a venue to facilitate repair of the family. Children may remain in the priut for as long as necessary but not more than one year. However, if a child needs to remain longer, Makarich will do his best to argue the case with the city bureaucracy.

Alla related something of the history of conflict between the child welfare authorities and priutye. "The city has an investment in traditional orphanages—*dietskiy doma*—and has strongly fought priutye because they represent a successful alternative. In fact, a year ago city authorities forced all the children then living in St. Petersburg priutye into dietskiy doma."

"A disaster," Alla said. "I just wept."

The critical difference between the priutye and the dietskiy doma is that the former are smaller and more flexible, more likely to respond to the particular needs of each child and, most important, they do not sequester children from society but maintain them very much in the neighborhood and, indeed, the world. Where possible, contact with the family is maintained.

Most dietskiy doma provide schooling within their walls. Children in priutye, by contrast, continue in most cases to attend their own neighborhood school. They are thus able to maintain and develop relationships with non-institutionalized people—including those in their own families. Custody of the child in the dietskiy doma is transferred to the City of St. Petersburg and lost to the family. With priutye, care and custody remain with the parents.

"Priutye," she said, "represent works in progress. Dietskiy doma tend to be points of no return."

"Unfortunately," Alla continued, "priutye are by law required to keep children for no longer than one year. We do everything we can to hold on to them for as long as is necessary. But we are usually overruled. However, we go right ahead and apply for special dispensation for as many children as we believe require it. It is a continuing battle. The City of St. Petersburg gets sick of dealing with us because by our keeping the children from their dietskiy doma we are in effect declaring such institutions to be the failures that indeed they are.

"Children coming out of Almus," Alla, explained, "do much better personally and in their school work than do children in dietskiy doma. Oddly, this is one of the factors that motivates attacks from the City. If our children had done poorly, they would have loved us."

- - - - - - - - - - - - - - - - -

The evening was spent with the two Serogias, the older street kid and the younger pain-in-the-neck. They played computer games in my kitchen. The older one muscled out all others who wished to play. I spoke to him about this a number of times but to no avail. Finally, he left to help supervise uborka in his Mafioso style. He hauled kids to their jobs, lifted them bodily and carried them, squirming, to their mops and buckets.

- - - - - - - - - - - - - - - - -

It is 10:30 PM. I didn't allow the children to play on the computer tonight so I bribed them with peanuts as I ushered them out the door. That got rid of them and the peanuts.

- - - - - - - - - - - - - - - - -

Another of those meetings about uborka took place with kids taking jobs as Ministers of This or That. It strikes me as a mildly inspired program idea. But the kids give it a higher rating. They were completely into the whole thing. The meeting was punctuated by shouting "*Da!*" or "*Nyet!*" when something came to a vote. Everyone participated. They jumped up and down waving their arms in the air when something went their way. Democracy is well established in this corner of Mother Russia.

I am impressed with how little serious conflict there appears to be within the group, none at all in fact is visible between children and adults. There is hardly any complaining or whining. Instead, there is a pervasive spirit of cooperation and good will. Even the teenagers for whom the program does not seem particularly well suited seem just as enthusiastic as the younger ones. Lena, for example, fully involved with adolescent issues, is an active participant in the democratic process.

- - - - - - - - - - - - - - - - -

Evening. Past eleven. I walk to the staff kitchen down the hall to return my tea cup.

"Bob! Bob!" comes Anya's alpha voice as I pass her room. "Go to sleep," I whisper.

On the way back, it's "Bob! Bob!" again. I tiptoe into the room. "Peanuts!" she commands. Her two roommates, sister Sashinka and their friend, Lyubishka, want peanuts, too.

"No more," I say. "They're all gone. Good night, girls. Time for sleep." I give each a kiss on the forehead. It is too late for peanuts. There will be peanuts tomorrow.

- - - - - - - - - - - - - - - - -

Morning. Three girls are in my room singing into the tape recorder. Despite the familiar scene—or more likely because of it—I have become old hat. I am no longer the main source of amusement in this place nor am I even an object of curiosity. I have become furniture. Kids come and go. Life swirls around me.

I took my breakfast alone for the first time. It wasn't that the kids were avoiding me. They all chirped, "Good morning, Bob" and "Good appetite" with customary cheeriness. It was just that they now take me for granted with not so much as a nod and then turn their attention to friends. I am left to my literary work I have always claimed I wanted to do.

I don't feel sorry for myself. Not me. It is good to sit back and watch the passing scene without being on stage.

- - - - - - - - - - - - - - - - -

I announced my interest in interviewing all vospitatilye who wished to volunteer. There was to be no list of questions. I would just let people talk. Irina Mikhailovna was the first to my door. Irina Mikhailovna is a stout, middle aged woman who dyes her hair an unlikely off-blond color, almost orange. She was born in 1940.

In 1948, under Stalin, my father was arrested and given a twenty-year sentence. To this day, I don't know what he was accused of. I doubt if my mother ever learned either. Thanks to Khrushchev, my father was released and rehabilitated in 1955, but he died soon afterward of cancer.

Things were bad under the Communists. They were destroying us, turning us into a colorless people. But at least then everybody was guaranteed an education. There were programs for children and places for them to live. Now our country is going through an unbelievable disaster. Perhaps I should say, "yet another unbelievable disaster." It is worse now than it was right after the war.

There are many, many children like these two little fellows over there who can't read or write and who have no home. Nobody knows how many there are.

The trouble is that our government is trying to change things too fast. It won't work. Look at China. They are moving slowly. They still have Communism but they have capitalism, too, and they are prospering. Their government is probably honest but ours is run by crooks, by criminals who don't know a thing about economics. Somebody up there should have studied the subject.

- - - - - - - - - - - - - - - -

Dima, a consulting psychiatrist for Vrachi Mira, is a young, informal man with a humorous face. Kids like him.

"What issues," I asked, "do you see in the use of mental health services here?"

My main concern is that vospitatilye tend to use psychiatric consultation as a punishment, a way of controlling behavior. They call the child "crazy" and threaten to send him or her to a psychiatrist if they don't cooperate. Or they will hand a difficult child over to the psychiatrist and assume that their responsibility is over.

My task as I see it is to interview new kids when they come into the priut, to observe them while they live here and to consult with the staff about them. I also dispense medications when it seems that they might be useful. I do some short term psychotherapy using methods such as Gestalt and Neurolinguistic Programming.

- - - - - - - - - - - - - - - -

My able young translator, Anya, helped me talk with two more Almus children, the older Andrei and Lena, both teenagers.

Andrei, 14

I've been here for a half year. I like it. It's been good for me. I like it because I can go to school and I can talk and play with other kids. And it's helping me study. There are some vospitatilye who help me with my math and my Russian. They tutor me on subjects I never studied because I was sick. I had problems with my hands, sort of like arthritis. I couldn't hold a knife and a fork—my mother had to feed me—and I couldn't study because I couldn't hold a pen. Now I'm better.

I'm here because my mother doesn't have a propiska (residence permit). We lost our apartment. When we moved, somebody lied to us. I don't really understand it but somehow we lost everything, our apartment, our propiska: everything. Now my mother lives with her boyfriend but they have only one room so they put me here.

I have a father, too. He is in Moscow and has a new family. I can't live there because of his wife but I do hear from him. We have a good relationship.

I want to be a cabinet maker when I grow up.

I get along with everybody and make friends easily. My only problem I have with this priut is that they lock the doors to the outside. If it were open, nobody would smoke in the toilet and nobody would run away through the widows. My friends and I do that every day. When I take off, I just go for a walk in the park and come right back.

Better than locking the kids in would be to leave the door open. Nobody would run away and the vospitatilye would be nicer to the kids. Some of them say really insulting things to us, like "You're sick in the head."

Some of the vospitatilye are better than others. The shift on duty now is the best. If we get punished, all they usually do is lock us in our rooms for maybe two hours or we get prohibited from watching TV or something like that. No big deal.

Sex and drugs? We never have discussions about things like that except with each other. But we've talked about AIDS with the medical workers downstairs.

We do talk about economics. When I get money, I buy cigarettes. Then I get a lecture from the vospitatilye on how to spend money wisely. I can earn all I need by cleaning the rooms and washing the floor and the toilets. Kids get paid for cleaning up this place. But they won't pay of you don't do a good job. I always do.

They have a children's court here for when somebody uses really bad words. Prizes are given for the best rooms. They give people a flower or something.

- - - - - - - - - - - - - - - - -

Lena, 14

I've been here since October. I like it. It is like home. I like everything about it.

I am here with Losha, my little brother, because our father is in hospital. My mother couldn't take care of us because she lost her parental rights. I was eight at the time. She drank a lot and often left us unsupervised. She hit us, too.

My father has tuberculosis. I worry about him.

I would like to be a vospitatilnitsa when a grow up. I like children very much. I'd like to be a baker, too. A baker and a vospitatilnitsa. But you have to go to school and study to be a vospitatilnitsa and I do only so-so in school.

They don't do sex education here and if they did, I wouldn't go. I know more about it than they do. I learned it in a class in school. I know about AIDS, too.

I don't agree with locking kids up in their rooms. If I were running this place, I wouldn't lock children up. I would give them more time to watch TV.

I can talk with the vospitatilye any time I want. But if I don't get along with an adult who is punishing me unfairly and I can't do anything about it, I just take the punishment and go to sleep in the locked room.

I could talk with the priut psychologist but I don't because I don't need to—I have a vospitatilnitsa I can tell about my problems any time I want to.

I love having little kids living here with us. It is good to have them around.

- - - - - - - - - - - - - - - - -

The children are going to the famous Leningrad Circus tonight. They invited me to come along. *"Konyechno!"* Of course!

I met them at the theater. Twelve children came accompanied by two vospitatilye. It happened to be the younger Serogia's thirteenth birthday. I bought him a fancy bar of candy. He took a bite right away then solemnly broke off little pieces and distributed them to his friends.

The show was wonderful. There were amazing acrobats plus two brilliant clowns, Sasha and Serogia, and performances by an unlikely array of animals including yaks, hedge-hogs, and a llama in addition to the usual horses, a bear, a tiger, monkeys, and myriad dogs.

The children loved every bit of it and were sky high when we headed home on the Metro. Young Sashas and Serogias invaded the subway car. Passengers smiled, dimly amused, but also disapproving probably of Tatiana Igor'ievna and me since we were the adults in nominal charge, responsible for this savage horde and were doing nothing to contain it.

We didn't get home until well after ten. We ate a late supper. The kids did not get to sleep until well after eleven. As I was nodding off, their racing and shouting through the halls threatened to keep me awake. But I pulled the blankets up over my head and fell into the deepest oblivion.

It is past noon. Most children are in school but a few of the older boys are hanging around. They sit in my kitchen office as I type. Some are drawing with crayons, others are flipping through my dictionary and still others are listening to rock music on my tape recorder.

Serogia, the quintessential street kid, sits beside me. He is curled up under my left arm with his head draped over the top of the cushion, almost asleep. Like a baby.

I have also seen Serogia become a monstrous bully when he wants something. He shoves other kids out of his way, especially little ones, and snatches things from them often with a cunning smile as if to say, "Can't you take a joke?" He is a curious mix of baby and thug.

Again after lunch, Serogia strode into my room without so much as a hello. He does that often, sometimes to my considerable irritation. Most other kids don't bother me so much but with Serogia, intrusion into my space is a prelude to being devoured. The boy has a sense neither of property, propriety nor boundaries.

He flops onto my kitchen chair. Silent. Like a rock.

Then: "I want to play on your computer," he says. "Five minutes only. Please"

"No, Serogia. I am going leave soon. Sorry." Then, attempting to change the subject, I ask, "What are your plans for the afternoon?"

"Nothing."

"Tomorrow?"

"Nothing."

"Do you have a job?"

"No."

"Do you go to school?"

"No."

"Why not?"

"I don't want to."

- - - - - - - - - - - - - - - -

There's a new kid, Tolya. He is a tall, intelligent fourteen-year-old. But, like Serogia, he bosses little kids around with no regard to their wishes, all the while smiling, a false advertisement of good will. He snatches things right out from under the smallest, weakest, and most passive. Neither he nor Serogia will share anything without firm pressure to do so from the grownup in charge.

One may imagine traces in these boys of the Brutal Father no doubt much like their own, the man they are all too likely to become.

But let us not lose sight of the other fathers in this world. Just before lunch, I noticed Sasha, the vospitatel, sitting in the television room. The box was shut of, silent and gray. Sasha was playing a game of chess with the ten-year-old Tolya—not the bossy fourteen-year-old one. Both Sasha and Tolya were deep in thought, an idealized portrait of father and son.

- - - - - - - - - - - - - - - - - -

Last night, the vospitatilye held a meeting with the children during which they bawled them out most effectively. Two boys had been caught smoking inside the priut and the older Serogia was found to have had a racket going in which he forced younger children to give him all their dining room food. He amassed quite a store in his room. Other house problems included the fact that everyone had gotten lax with uborka and were not getting to bed on time. Much tightening up was in order. It was a tough meeting but, sprinkled within theatrical vospitatilye outrage, there was considerable good humor.

Meeting over, the kids snapped into their uborka and were bed before ten. Impressive.

However, the meeting, although a good show, was all top down. It was the *staff* that *made* the kids get their acts together. And, although some of the kids had a great deal to say, what transpired could hardly have been called a "dialogue." It was an expert chewing out.

If this were a family, whether natural or constructed, and if vospitatilye did not change every day, perhaps a more collaborative culture might have evolved. There are certainly the makings here for collaboration in the very warmth and irreverence of the meeting.

In the spirit of the occasion, I distributed bedtime *pechen'iy*—cookies—to all those who popped into my room to say "goodnight." I handed out more than was good for them ... seconds, thirds, fourths, fifths ...

- - - - - - - - - - - - - - - -

I am making a big thing in my mind about leaving and so are the vospitatilye and the children. "When will you come back?" they ask.

The staff gave me a lovely book that I don't know how to read plus a cake.

"We will cry when you go," Tatiana Nikolaevna said. It was like the leave-taking scenes in Chekhov plays. Good-byes and more good-byes and good-byes.

This whole remarkable adventure will be over in only a few days. I will miss these people.

- - - - - - - - - - - - - - - -

The room was full of kids as I finished packing. Vitalik made a big show of trying to climb into my duffel bag.

"I'll bring you with me and give you to some American. You will be a souvenir from Russia!" I said.

"But I can't speak English."

"So what? I am in Russia and I can't speak Russian."

"Yes, you *can!* I *heard* you!"

Spasibo, Vitalik ….

- - - - - - - - - - - - - - - - -

The younger Misha danced around the room chanting, "Fuck you!" and "Kiss my ass!" in his best English.

The younger Serogia flicked his cigarette lighter. He showed everyone who cared to watch that he could put his hand through the flame and it didn't get burned. "Give that to me, *durok* (jerk)," I said firmly. But he ran from me. I have no power. I am no vospitatel.

New kids joined us, thirteen-year-old Lena and Yura, and six-year-old Dimuchka. Some who were in the priut when I first arrived, Artyom, for example, are now gone on to dietskiy doma.

Alpha Anya tried on my enormous backpack. She collapsed under its weight, giggling. Sashinka, her sister, perched on the dresser, laughed herself silly.

Losha demanded more cookies. "They are all gone," I said. "Sorry."

"No fair," he said.

1999

A terrible sadness hangs over Peter's fabled metropolis.

Surely I am offering a trite observation but it does reflect something real. The lofty imperial architecture in Center City Petersburg is one thing but the uncollected trash on the grass between crumbling cement high rise project building on the outskirts is something quite different, no worse than New York City to be sure, and quite possibly better, but hardly attractive.

Have things slipped in the months that I have been gone or does it only seem that way? Perhaps my perception is distorted because I was last here in midwinter when the mud and trash were buried in the snow. Now, in the full bloom of springtime, everything is revealed in all its shabbiness. The world has awakened to neglect.

It is unfortunate that none of the children I knew from my earlier visit are still here except for one guy, the adolescent Tolya. All the rest are back with their families or in orphanages, the dietskiy doma. The staff hasn't changed much except for the addition of a vospitatilnitsa.

I ran into a new girl. Her name is Sveta. She is sixteen years old but could pass for twenty-five. I assumed that she was the new vospitatilnitsa. Anyone could have made that mistake. Sveta has a mature, responsible manner and takes a big sister role with the younger children who obviously respect her.

Her parents, she told me, were alcoholics. She was brought up by a grandmother. Sadly, the grandmother died five years ago. Since then Sveta has been living in each of three institutions for children. She thinks Almus is by far the best of these.

- - - - - - - - - - - - - - - - -

The vospitatilye welcomed me with considerable warmth and invited me to tea. Priut Almus is going well, they explained, but life in Russia is very bad, worse than ever. People have become ever poorer. As a consequence, more and more children require care.

Besides having forgotten most of my meager Russian, I can no longer remember anybody's name. But slowly, all too slowly, they are drifting back to awareness. By the time I left last year, I had achieved a fragile grasp on all of them. Now I must begin again.

Tatiana Igor'ievna takes me aside. She has something to tell me. (Well, there! I *do* remember *one* name,"Tatiana Igor'ievna." I have taken the liberty of calling her, "Tanya.") Tanya told me that she read a translation of my notes on last year's visit and thought it "an important piece of work." (What a fine woman!)

"Thank you very much, Tanya," I said. She added that my arguments in favor of tactile contact—hugs, embraces, brushing hair—with the kids was something she especially agreed with. The translation of the title the Russians gave the piece was, "Touching."

"But I must go back to the kids now." Off she went.

I handed a copy of the translated report to Tolya, the reticent fifteen-year-old boy I met last year. He is a bright fellow and showed an interest in the subject. I believe he will read it.

Why is Tolik (a diminutive of Tolya, in turn a diminutive of Anatolii) still here? What are the circumstances? How was it arranged? Children normally are obliged to move on after only a few months—a year at most. Makarich probably hassled the city functionaries enough to make it happen. An exception.

Tolik arrived for the first time during my first visit fourteen months ago. Almus has done well by him. He is more confident now, less reserved, less clingy and better able to interact with other children.

This current bunch of kids, like last year's, gather in my sitting room. They play with the computer and we take pictures; the usual routine. I hand out Cabot Creamery Vermont cheddar cheese slices. They are individually wrapped in plastic. The children consider the wrapping a distinct plus, possibly more valuable than the cheese itself.

Introductions? Well, we have Sasha and Zhenya, two eight-year-old boys whose names are now firmly in my head. But I am sure I will soon confuse them even though they don't look at all alike. Then there is Alyona who wears lipstick and tries to look sexy at the age of twelve; and eight-year-old Mariana who is smiley and quick-witted.   She instructs the older kids on playing computer games.

It is impossible to ignore thirteen-year-old female Pasha, the one with the loud, rasping voice.   Pasha is a tough kid but has a look of vulnerability about her.   Next let us meet the two Andrushkas, one a teenaged boy who wears a mask of strained cheerfulness, and the other, a shy, reticent ten- or eleven-year-old fellow with blond hair and a round, inscrutable face.

We had dinner together consisting of kasha, cutlets, bread, butter and tea, a healthy, well-prepared meal.

- - - - - - - - - - - - - - - - -

After dinner, a variety of children wander into my sitting room again.   I hand each a Cabot Creamery coloring book and a set of Ben and Jerry's crayons.

More kids arrive.   I distribute stuff to anybody who asks—and ask they do once they see what the first bunch of kids got.   I know I am overdoing this but can't stop.   I go through my baggage for more gifts but just then vospitatilnitsa Irina Ivanovna pokes her head in at the door and, with a disarming smile, tells me that she does not think it is right to give any presents at all to the children.   I cannot entirely follow her argument but figured that she is probably right for reasons one can well imagine.   Gifts commodify relationships.   The giving of concrete, manufactured objects—even food— creates a frantic, pot-latch atmosphere.

I wish I could have understood her exact words.   But, whatever it is precisely that she had in mind, I am sure it was sensible.   Beaten down children whether in Russia or elsewhere are not used to receiving gifts. Who am I to change that? Worse, my offerings make me look like a big shot and put the vospitatilye at a disadvantage since they have little to give beyond themselves and their services.

On the other hand, an argument could be made *for* the giving of gifts, particularly if the giver is an exception, a guest, and not likely to set an institutional precedent. If the gift is small and symbolic rather than lavish, if what is given has neither violent nor obscene connotations, and if everyone is given something approximately equal in value, why *shouldn't* children, especially poor children, be given something, and end up *owning* something personal, something not the property of the entire group?

But, as my wife says, I *do* tend to create chaos in children and should learn to control myself.

This year I promise to go easy on Almus. I promise to observe unobtrusively and consult sensitively. I will not rile up the children. I will not make things hard for vospitatilye whose lives are hard enough as it is. I will be restrained in the giving of gifts. I will respect all rules and customs.

- - - - - - - - - - - - - - - - - -

It is 9:15 p.m. I am typing. The door to my sitting room is open. Kids are racing up and down the halls except for those who are watching a violent American television program in the sitting room two door down.

It is the end of the shift. One of the vospitatilye is about to go home. She sings out, "Goodnight, Bob. See you on Tuesday. Have a nice time."

My sitting room is a social center. I give out mixed signals on purpose ... more or less. I do want the kids to visit and I want to observe them but after a while I want to ease them out.

Sasha wanders in and I give him a handful of peanuts. But I also tell him that I am busy. After collecting his loot, he dances out into the hallway. But soon he's back. I then hand him a Cabot Creamery coloring book and a package of Ben and Jerry crayons. He colors vigorously.

Bribery. Unmitigated bribery.

Alyona enters. She's twelve. She munches the peanuts I offer her. Then she goes to her own room to do her homework but soon returns and continues her work in my sitting room. Quietly.

Alyona's background, she said, is German. "*Güten abend, Bob*," she says.

"*Güten abend, Alyona.*"

Mila, age thirteen, joins us. She carries herself with graceful, boyish athleticism. She gazes at the notes I am working on. Little Mariana sits close beside me. She recognizes her name in Latinate letters. Nadya, age seven, is sleepy. She yawns and rubs her eyes. She folds herself under the arm of Irina Ivanovna, the vospitatilnitsa who has joined us a few moments ago and who is now sitting very close to Nadinka (a diminutive of Nadya). She brushes Nadinka's hair slowly, tenderly, sensually, maternally.

And so it continued for the longest while. Gradually everyone went their way. The older children gathered with the vospitatilye in the staff kitchen as I finished this entry. It was past eleven when I finally got to bed. I could hear them all talking and laughing in the staff kitchen next door.

Their sounds revived me. I rose up to join them. We chatted for almost an hour. We spoke in Russian, English and a scattering of German. It is now a quarter to twelve and I am in bed again, rapidly dropping off.

Children are always welcome in the staff kitchen. The evident warmth between the children and staff is the very finest thing about this place. I must learn more about that. Why else did I come?

- - - - - - - - - - - - - - - -

7:30 AM. I unlock my door and open it wide thus advertising that I am prepared to receive visitors. Losha, fourteen, slick, aggressive, funny, sweet, pokes in his head. "Good morning," he says in heavily accented but otherwise impeccable English. He knows a half dozen English words, "good" and "morning" are among the few that are not obscene.

En route to the bathroom, Alyona shuffles by in her pajamas.

- - - - - - - - - - - - - - - -

Irina Nikolaevna will be on duty today as Irina Ivanovna's shift is done. She is headed home. I am aware of at least one more Irina who works here but I can't remember which one she is. Tatiana Igor'ievna will be off duty in a moment and Tatiana Viktorovna will be on. And so it goes.

Natalia Nikolaevna came into my suite and welcomed me back with genuine feeling.

Klavdia Aleksandrovna, who was the Almus in-house tutor last year, has been promoted. She is now "Director of the Second Floor." She had the job last year *de facto* but not *de jure*.

It is a quarter past nine. Tatiana Igor'ievna and Irina Ivanovna invite me to pre-breakfast tea. I contribute a hunk of Cabot, Vermont, cheddar cheese. The women ask me questions in a manner that demands an answer but all too often I cannot understand them nor do I have the skill to form an adequate response.

- - - - - - - - - - - - - - - - -

Ten o'clock. Breakfast. Afterward, a bunch of kids gathered in my sitting room for more computer games, coloring and hanging out. They stayed for over an hour.

"Only ten more minutes on the computer, Pashinka," I said. "Then it's over—*svo!*—because I need to get back to my writing work."

After ten minutes Pasha was still at it so I made a big show of grabbing the computer out of her hands. I was silly, not angry. She laughed.

"But before I can work," I said as I shut down the machine, "I need a walk. Anybody want to come with me?"

Mariana and Mila squealed that they needed a walk, too. So, off we went.

"Take us to the *Tarzanka*," Mila begged. I had no idea what she meant. "Sure," I said, assuming that a Tarzanka was perhaps some sort of candy or an ice cream store, "but unfortunately I have no rubles with me."

It turned out that rubles were not required. "Tarzanka" is a Tarzan swing, a long rope that hangs from a tall tree in a nearby playground. Children grab it, climb it, and swing wildly into space giving forth with a mighty "Yaaaaaaa!" exactly like Tarzan. Mila scrambled up the rope in an instant and did exactly that.

"Are you a girl or a boy?" a little girl asked athletic Mila.

"A girl," she answered with contempt. Her gender, she thought, is obvious to any idiot. The fact is that she does look to be on the boyish side. But she views herself as fully feminine though hardly a creature of fashion, frills or makeup.

Next, with Mila's help, little Mariana also swung from the rope but far more quietly and judiciously.

As we headed back to the priut, the three of us held hands and skipped along. The neighborhood no longer seemed as dismal as it had yesterday. Now, in the company of these two girls, it had become beautiful.

Yet, in retrospect there is certainly something repellent about high-powered electric lines that hang from an endless line of tall, spindly towers along the middle of an otherwise pleasant boulevard. In Soviet times such icons of industrial progress reflected a Socialist dream. Nineteenth-century America was similar. This St.

Petersburg moonscape is therefore no more dispiriting than Elizabeth, New Jersey, or Gary, Indiana.

- - - - - - - - - - - - - - - -

Mikhail Makarievich, the founder and director of Almus, long since out of hospital, arrives in my kitchen/salon to introduce himself. The famous Makarich at last! Eschewing small talk, he announces that on Tuesday a conference is to be held here at Almus to which psychologists and psychiatrists from all over Russia have been invited.

"You," he says, "are invited, too."

"I am more than happy to attend," I say. "I am very pleased to meet you," I add.

Mikhail Makarievich is called "Makarich" by his friends. Russian men are often referred to by a short form of their otchestvo.

Makarich—I presume to be among his friends although I do not yet know him—projects a theatrical intensity that makes him a natural with children. He is middle-aged, balding, and has piercing brown eyes and a brown mustache. He leans forward as he speaks. His words pour forth rapidly. It is not possible for me to follow so I observe him. He smiles a lot but it is the ironic smile of the Russian intellectual rather than the chuckle-headed guffaw so common in our country. He is, I thought, undeniably an interesting fellow, challenging but oddly shy.

Makarich left my room as suddenly as he entered and with neither comment nor ceremony.

Fifteen minutes later he showed up again, this time with a certain Sergei in tow, a young man who is studying electrical engineering at St. Petersburg University. As a child, Sergei was a resident at Almus. He is now a successful alum, having both an education and a job.

Makarich explained that Sergei has studied English and would be pleased to translate our conversation. As it turned out, Sergei's command of my language was not that much better than mine was of his. Our conversation ended with the promise that we would meet again soon.

- - - - - - - - - - - - - - - -

Children are in my sitting room again, coloring. Among them are Lena and Mila both of whom, I would have thought, have far too much energy for sedentary work.

The little boys, Sasha and Zhenya, more energetic still, are coloring furiously, joyously, chaotically. Hey, *Bop*!" Zhenya shouts mispronouncing my name in a way that pleases me. "Do you have presents for me today?"

"Of *course* I do, Zhenka, That coloring book you are drawing on is a gift from me to *you*!"

"Spacibo!" he screams.

Lena hands her coloring book back to me. She wrote on it in carefully scripted Russian, "From Lena to Bob." I give her a hug and a kiss on the cheek.

- - - - - - - - - - - - - - - -

Sunday. Most of the kids are doing their mandated weekly uborka. It is a demanding activity but a few wily children manage to goof off by hanging around the edges, chatting and slithering off to my sitting room—making me complicit in their delinquency. Those who take it at all seriously and do a reasonably good job are paid a small amount for their efforts.

The television in the recreation room down the hall is blaring. I can't see what's happening from where I sit but I imagine a dozen transfixed children sprawled on the floor.

- - - - - - - - - - - - - - - -

Here in my mind's eye is how a residential institution for children could and should look even in the face of sorely limited resources:

- Art. There should be pictures, especially those made by the children, tacked onto every wall.

- Animals. Dogs are best but cats would be fine as would horses, donkeys, or pigs.

- Greenery. There should be green or flowering plants in every room.

- Light. Sunshine through billowing white curtains and reflected on bright colored walls.

- Low ceilings, sitting rooms, play rooms, and bedrooms large enough for no more than four children in each and containing well-designed boxes and shelves for personal belongings.

- A conveniently located snack kitchen replete with tea, lemon, and cookies.

- - - - - - - - - - - - - - - -

My camera was stolen! I carried it in my zippered bag where I thought it was safe. But there was no secure closing mechanism that might have foiled a thief, only the zipper. The thief unzipped it. How dumb of me. How Stupid. Stupid. Stupid. Stupid.

I know *exactly* when it happened. I had taken four Almus girls to the Lomonovskaya Metro station for ice cream after a group visit to center city.

There was a big crowd around the ice cream stand. People pressed in close on every side.

I felt a slight pushing sensation on my bag. I backed away, patting it down to make sure it was still there. It was but I did not check specifically for the camera. I gave the matter no further thought until I offered to take a picture of the girls eating ice cream. I reached into the bag for the camera. Gone!

The positive side is that it was, after all, an old camera, hardly a quality brand, a Ricoh SLR, not worth much. And I still have my wallet. And my passport. And my lap-top computer. And my life. But not my brains.

I am under stress. I am stressed by the Russian language. Living with all these great children is stressful. I have a headache. I need a nap. They don't serve coffee at Almus.

I had wanted to get money from the ATM machine at the Metro entrance surrounding which is a crowded marketplace. That was why I took the camera from around my neck and put it in the bag. I didn't want to attract thieves. It was the right instinct but the wrong bag. I should have had one with a clasp, not a zipper.

Back at Almus, the vospitatilye were sympathetic. "But that's Russia for you," Tatiana Viktorovna said with a sigh. "We have Mafias everywhere."

"It is not only in Russia that such things happen," I assured her. "It goes on in New York, too."

"Oh?" she said, sighing again as if to say, "The world is a dangerous place. But it is our fate to live in it."

- - - - - - - - - - - - - - - - -

The visit today to center city was intended to introduce the children to high culture. We boarded a tour bus to see the sights in Pushkina, Pushkin's home town. Today Russia is celebrating his two-hundredth birthday.

I understood little of what the guide said. She read rapidly from a script and made no effort to make herself comprehensible to us, her audience, a dozen Russian children and a foreign man.

Later, we stopped at a park to rest. The kids raced around and climbed onto the famous statue of Peter the Great on his high horse behind which, surrealistically, a formal wedding was taking place. The bride wore an elegant long, white gown and the groom a black tuxedo, white shirt, gold cufflinks, and black bow tie. They posed, kissing, for a photograph.

- - - - - - - - - - - - - - - - -

There are several new kids here who arrived since I did only a day ago. Now that I have finally memorized all the names, here are more to learn.

Little Yura, smart though he is, has an awful temper. He

flies off the handle with no apparent provocation. He cries and hits people at random, even his good friend, Andrei, who looks so much like him that I assumed they were brothers. A few minutes ago, completely out of the blue,Yura screamed and pummeled Andrei without mercy.

Fortunately, there were three vospitatilye with us on the excursion. They each spoke with Yura quietly while bathing him in sympathetic smiles. One vospitatilnitsa put her arm around his shoulder and led him gently back to the group.

Yura did finally get over the tantrum but his face remained red and sullen for a very long time.

- - - - - - - - - - - - - - - - -

Sometimes on our outings I worry that vospitatilye are not sufficiently attentive. I am not sure if they keep count or know for sure who is supposed to be in the group nor do they seem particularly intent on keeping everyone together.

We started off today at a fast clip and headed to the bus that was to take us to the Metro. But some children dawdled behind while others ran ahead. We didn't even all take the same paths through the housing project. Some sped across the lawn while some went on one walkway, some on another.

I asked a vospitatilnitsa—whom I shall not name—how many children we had with us. She wasn't sure, she confessed, but proceeded to count them in on her fingers as she caught sight of them. That was not easy to do because the kids were running this way and that.

"I believe there are eight," she said. I counted thirteen and pointed that out to her.

"Oh, yes. I know. That is *exactly* how many we have. Thirteen," she said.

Okay. Some Almus vospitatilye may be less than perfect on details but I have yet to see one lose her temper or threaten a kid. They manage to remain on an even keel throughout, supportive yet firm.

- - - - - - - - - - - - - - - - -

When Pasha, Lyuba, Alyona and Lena asked me for the ice cream that led to the theft of my camera, they asked me to buy an extra cone for a friend who was with them. She used to stay at Almus but now lives in an *internat* (boarding school) nearby. I made the purchase as requested and then proceeded to interview the girl without benefit of translator because none was around.

"Almus is great," she said. "But the internat is awful." I asked her to tell me more but she could not come up with examples.

"That's just what I think," she said. "That's the way it is."

- - - - - - - - - - - - - - - - -

I am struck by how naturally people from societies more traditional than ours handle children. I've noted this in both Haiti and in Russia. In both those countries there seems to be an unspoken assumption that the child will do the right thing in the end. Little is excused by psychic trauma nor by virtue of sad upbringings, nor are there threats of the "consequences" that we Americans find compelling.

On the other hand, it must be granted that children in Haiti and Russia are routinely beaten, sometimes savagely, and may be abandoned and abused in terrible ways. I am not arguing that parents in Russia and Haiti are better than their counterparts in the United States only that there are differences and that in some important respects sophisticated Americans do no better. Often we do worse.

Ours lapses, I think, are related to our belief in consequences. A "consequence" is an unfortunate market formulation, both Capitalist and Medieval. The idea is that if you want to do bad things, you may just so long as you are prepared to "pay" for the privilege. You may purchase the right to be a pig. In other countries, you simply behave. There is no tradeoff and no reward for your behavior because there is no possibility of doing otherwise, no punishment for doing wrong except banishment from the community. The task of the offender in such a case becomes reconciliation through penance or reparation.

Under the Tsars, people were banished for *behavioral* deviations. Under the Communists, it was often for unacceptable *thought* as well. There existed in Russia then and indeed exists to this day a culturally defined way of being to which most people accede. Such a consensus is not to be found in most of contemporary America … although it is alive and well in rural Vermont where policemen and social workers are rarely seen but where people help each other out with food baskets, barn-raisings and similar social offerings.

- - - - - - - - - - - - - - - -

Jeff, Vrachi Mira's St. Petersburg director, provided me with a translator, a real professional. Her name is "Assiya" short for "Anastasia." Her shortest name, used by friends and relatives, is "Assi," She permits me to call her that. Assi is in a St. Petersburg University program for translators. She is twenty-two years old, quick-witted, and given to stylish dress including dramatic black sweaters, short skirts and high heels, a far classier package than I am accustomed to.

With such help on board, I formulated a goal: Together we would interview *everyone* in Almus, kids and vospitatilye alike. I knew that there were some amazing stories here and, at the risk of tedium, I wanted to hear and record them all.

As we worked together, Assi frequently asserted herself. "I wouldn't put the question quite that way," she advised more than once. I invariably accepted her advice.

- - - - - - - - - - - - - - - -

An interview with Lyuba. Assi assisting.

Lyuba, who was here last year, is shy, a shyness enhanced by a certain unconscious charm. Although not overweight, she has a friendly, round face and her body has a butterball quality. She is well liked both by children and grownups. She tends not to put herself forward nor to make demands. When she believes that she is not good at something, she pulls back. When things don't go as she wants them to, her face assumes a look of annoyance rather than assertion, probably at herself. She accepts things as they are.

I've been living in Almus for two years. My mother and grandmother wanted to sell their apartment but they were cheated by some guy so now they have no apartment and no money. That's why I'm here.

My mom and my grandma come here to visit me a lot. My father lives with his mother, my other grandmother. He doesn't come to see me at Almus but I often go see him on weekends.

When we lost the apartment, my grandma talked with the Almus psychologists and asked them if they could keep me here for more than a year and they did. After this summer I will definitely be going home.

I miss home but I really like Almus. Everything here is good. I have a whole lot of friends. We get to go on walks and we go to museums and theaters and stuff like that. In my free time I like playing outside and making things with glass beads. It is a hobby called "finchka."

It's always fun here. I will really miss it when I go home.

I have a brother and a sister who are younger than me. My sister is eight and my brother is three. My sister lives with my father and my grandma. At first I lived there, too, but my father and my uncle drank and sometimes got into fights. So my other Grandma, my mother's mother, said she didn't want me living in a place like that so she took me to this priut. She wanted to take my sister out of there, too, but my other grandmother—my father's mother—went to court and got guardianship of me before my mother could.

- - - - - - - - - - - - - - - -

One of the last kids to leave my sitting room last night

was Yura, the little boy with the big temper. He sat for a long time quietly drawing picture after picture of me which he then handed over as gifts as he looked oddly embarrassed. Had he ever given anybody a gift before?

In one of his drawings I was portrayed as a placid-enough fellow. But I held two pistols, one in each hand. I told him that I thought it was really a portrait of himself. He disagreed.

Yura continued to play on my computer for a while and then, when a vospitatilnitsa came to tell him that it was time for bed, I gave him a bear hug as we walked together out the door. He accepted it and softly mumbled, "*Poka*," which means "See you later."

Mila was in the room then, too, as was Lena. Although these are active, outdoor girls, they assiduously colored and drew many pictures after which they handed them to me all enhanced with hearts, arrows and inscriptions such as, "To our friend" and "We love you."

- - - - - - - - - - - - - - - - -

Morning. My sitting room is filled with kids yet again, Yura, Mariana, Zhenya, Yulia, and Marina—a little girl I had not met before—plus Pasha, and Sveta. Alyona arrives as I write this. She is only twelve but she wears a long, dramatic skirt, a light green sweater and dark glasses. She looks very Hollywood.

They all want to play games on the computer but when I tell them I am working on my own stuff, they are content to sit and watch me, comment and ask questions. I can only understand some of what they say. I reply to the rest with a nod of the head or a hopeful *"Da"* or an occasional *"Nyet."*

These children aren't clingy. But they do thrive on attention. They don't compete with one another. It may be that these, my Almus kid friends, want nothing more than to be in the presence of a benign grownup. The staff here gives them generous portions of attention to be sure. But it tends to be on the instrumental side, oriented to matters of health or to a particular task: "Why don't you finish your kasha?" or "Aren't you feeling well?" or "Why did you cough?" or "Take your medicine!" or "Make your bed!"

These children have relatively little opportunity simply to sit in the presence of benign grownups, doing nothing and having nothing in particular to do.

- - - - - - - - - - - - - - - - -

The morning began with a conference on a topic that might be translated as "Helping Children Who Grow Up Without Families." About forty people came. Assi translated for me and, when it was my turn to speak, she translated my words for them, no doubt crafting significant improvements.

Although unprepared and muddled, I made a brief speech arguing for program-design as opposed to fretting about psychotherapy and psychopharmacology.

An expert on child sexual abuse said, "Most girls can take up to *two weeks* to get over sexual trauma!"

So ... the subject has hit the shores of Russia!

Assi and I left at the tea break.

- - - - - - - - - - - - - - - -

Psychopathology: Although there are refreshing exceptions, the tendency in the United States is to proceed on a case by case basis, staying clear of murky social and political matters. Our aim is to locate and isolate psychopathology thereby to excise or medicate it. There is some rhetoric but little done to address social, possibly etiological factors such as the weakening of family bonds, the increase in social isolation, or the sexualization of advertising and the media. Of course, there are exceptions but what I am describing is surely what dominates our thinking. Through our courts we seek to identify a perpetrator and chastise him through fines, restrictions, jailing or isolation. We also seek to compensate the victim, through the application of salve and cliches.

Do we ever seriously consider why some people rather than others are given to abuse? Did their formative years lack in affection? Was the atmosphere at home one of desperation and chaos? Were loving and battering somehow confounded? Did closeness fuse with sadism?

All of us when young, require a parental embrace. If it is rarely given or if warmth and arousal become impossible to disentangle, one may expect to see a growing child at risk for emptiness rather than fulfillment, physical power instead of strength of character, and prurience in place of affection.

When society collapses, when hope dims, when food, shelter, and responsibility fade, the soul shrivels.

- - - - - - - - - - - - - - - -

Lyuba and Yulia beg me to take more pictures of them.

I suggested that because of the poor light in the house, it might be best to do the job outdoors. We ended with seven kids, vospitatilnitsa Tanya Igor'ievna, and me all romping the neighborhood together. We walked first to a nearby playground that featured an impressive jungle-gym and a wonderfully dangerous seesaw. The Communists were big on playgrounds. Playgrounds are everywhere in Russia. A plus for the Soviets!

I took many pictures with my replacement camera, a used Pentax SLR, old but good, definitely superior to the stolen Ricoh.

- - - - - - - - - - - - - - - -

The green grass rectangles between the looming concrete buildings of the high-rise housing complex form arrow-straight walking paths that bespeak rectitude. To tread impulsively across the lawn instead of following the righteous path is to deviate. On the other hand, to follow the correct path is to go out of one's way, to make a right angle where an impulsive, irrational hypotenuse would be more practical. The apartment complex greens are therefore crisscrossed by thoughtless people, *narodni'y*, ordinary Russians who, in the face of planners, Communist and Capitalist, trample lawns at will, oblivious to the designs of rational planners.

- - - - - - - - - - - - - - - -

Vrachi Mira has given me a task. I am to help bring the mental health workers and vospitatilye up to "western standards." I am to teach scientific psychology. By that

I think they mean Western fashions in psychodiagnosis and psychotherapy. Unfortunately, I am congenitally unfashionable. I think Russians do fine with their children. Priut Almus is a case in point. I am aware of nothing like Almus in the United States. My own goal here is otherwise. It is to get the information flowing the other direction, from Russia to America.

Will Vrachi Mira tolerate a consultant who proclaims, "I have nothing to teach you. I am here to learn?"

But if they ask me how to become effective in their work with children, I shall do my best to answer.

Answer: One must look in two directions simultaneously, toward the child and toward his or her entire context that includes family, community, economics, politics, and history. Then the child we shall see is both a *particular* child and a *modal* child, each positioned to illuminate the other.

Who is the modal child?

The modal child is not one beset with pathology. He or she is merely okay in the sense of being typical, neither crazy nor sane, neither happy nor sad, neither rich nor poor, neither delinquent nor law-abiding—but with the curious potential to become any or all of these singly or at once. The modal child may help us consider what we must provide every particular child, and guides us to what each particular child deserves independent of his or her unique history, genome, or state of psyche.

The Modal Child requires ...

- A Stable, Benign if not entirely Loving, Network of Human Relationships

- A Pervasive Climate of Safety

- One or more Significant Others who care if he or she lives or dies

- Recognition as an Individual, not unique but with Laudable Attributes

- The sense of being a Member of the Human Community

- An ongoing Celebration of Personal Growth

- Tasks and Challenges: Hurdles, Physical and Mental, that are Possible to Overcome

- A climate of Wit, Delight in the Absurd, and Infinite Patience for things as they are

- A climate of Commitment to Passionate but Thoughtful Struggle to Change Things for the Better

If a setting contained such qualities, would that not facilitate the growth of the particular child—and adult—regardless of psychopathology or circumstances? Might not such attributes prove curative for those of us who are ill and enhancing for the everyone else?

A program for particular young children that is designed to prevent the worst might well consist in nothing more than the provision of food, drink, clothing, a home, constancy, an ample lap to rest on, and no more interpersonal hassle than can be contended with.

Whether as parents or vospitatilye, while children are in our care, we have the duty, indeed the privilege, to raise them as well as we can.

Last night Natalia Nikolaevna and I took a group of nine children for a long walk. We strolled along the bank of the Neva, past the high rise *Rechnaya Gostinitsa* (River Hotel). We ran and we skipped. The never-ending, gloaming of the St. Petersburg spring lay in horizontal splendor. I took photographs, portraits of individuals as well as group shots for which the giddy children posed with their arms around each other.

I gave shoulder rides. My first customer was seven-year-old Nadinka who argued her case irresistibly. Two days ago when I tossed her onto my shoulders for the first time, she was frightened. But today she is into it. As for me, after a dozen kids, I have a backache.

Anna Sergeevna, who worked for me last year as a translator, is sixteen. She is fluent in English and visited this evening to ask if I needed her to help me interview children.

Of course. But first, I asked her to tell me about herself:

Anna Sergeevna is stylish, poised and serious. Although still in secondary school, she could easily pass for a university student.

I've been studying English for seven years, ever since I was nine. I studied at the Technical College of Commerce and Management. My eventual profession will be computer engineer. I love computer games.

I have a good family that includes my mother, my

grandmother, and my dog.   I also have a cat but I especially love my dog. My hobby is to take care of my dog and to study English.   When I have spare time, I read English books.

It was my mother's idea that I learn English. When I was a little girl my mother decided that that's what I should do. I found that liked it and I began to study it without any pressure from her.   It is my dream to work as a translator in English speaking countries.

After I finish technical school, I will go to university and continue my studies in English and computer engineering.

* * *

Anna Sergeeovna helped me interview Nadinka, the girl who rode on my shoulders.

Nadya, age 7. Nadinka is chatty, engaging and popular. She is cute and no doubt well aware of it. Although the youngest person in Almus, children even two and three years older seek her company.

I like it here because the food is very good and, if you ask permission, you can get to do what you want. I also like the kids. I have lots of friends.

Galina Mikhailovna and Maria Vasilyevna are my favorite vospitatilye. They are very nice.

I like to play games. Mostly I like to play with Barbie. I am not very good at jump rope but I am learning.

I've been here two or maybe three months. At home I have a mother, a father and a brother. My mom and dad don't have work. They don't have money to feed *us. That's why I'm here. But they take me to visit them at home almost every weekend. I miss being home but I like it here, too.*

My brother is at an internat (boarding school). He also gets to go home on weekends.

I have no suggestions for making Almus better. It is great just as it is!

- - - - - - - - - - - - - - - - -

As we walked along the street this afternoon,Yura, the fellow prone to temper tantrums, made a bouquet of green leaves and ferns that he presented to Natalia Nikolaevna, a vospitatilnitsa especially attentive to the needs of the children. "*Molodiets,*" (good boy) she purred. She accepted the gift with effusive thanks. This is the second time I've seen Yura give a special gift to someone. The first time it was to me.

- - - - - - - - - - - - - - - -

Yesterday I watched as Dr. Alla Pavlovna palpated little Sasha's naked torso. His face radiated pleasure. Her cool stethoscope touched first his chest, now his belly. Her magical hands caressed his back. Her dancing fingers hammered, touched, tested, here and then there, always gently, ever so gently.

"What a nice boy, what a *good* boy!" she purred. "*Molodiets.*" She smiled. It was a warm smile yet slightly touched by that familiar shadow of irony I've heard before in the timbre of her voice. I wonder if Sasha could hear it, too.

"Sasha is in very good health," she concluded. "There

was no reason to expect otherwise." This was a routine examination. All the children in Almus are seen regularly by doctors and dentists.

Alla Pavlovna's English has much improved during the past year while my poor Russian limps along. I seldom conjure the right word still; the niceties of grammar continue to escape me. I open my mouth and discordant sounds fly out of their own accord. No *molodiets* here.

- - - - - - - - - - - - - - - -

The Almus boys know a few English words. "Fuck you, *bitch!*" they exclaim with accompanying expression and grimace. They learn these things from Russian MTV. Not from me.

And German words, too. Yesterday, one boy barked hilariously, *"Alle Jüden im Wagonen!"* All Jews into the railway cars!

"Tyi ochen glup'yi mal'chik," I said. "You are a very stupid boy."

- - - - - - - - - - - - - - - -

I play-wrestled Yura in the hall, a dangerous thing to do. He tried to punch me in the genitals—hard—but I backed off just in time and held him tightly across the chest in a bear hug.

He melted. Yura is extremely volatile but he responds well to any suggestion that he is liked. I've taken many pictures of him but it is never enough. "Photo! Bob! Now! *Please!*" he commands when we pass each other in the hallway.

Before he discovered that I bought a replacement camera, his approach had been, "Dollar! Give me dollar! *Please!*" followed by *"Fucking Bitch!"* in perfect English, grinning while awaiting my response.

"*Durok!*" I said. Fool.

- - - - - - - - - - - - - - - - -

Yura stalks into my room. "*Please*, Bob, *one* more photo. This is the *last* time."

He shows me a one-ruble coin and hands it to me. I had jokingly demanded money from him as he had from me. It seems that he took me seriously. A ruble is now worth about four cents.

"See? I can pay you," he says.

I shove the coin back into his hand. "Keep your money, my friend. I'll take one more picture of you. But no computer games today. I'm working." I pose him at the computer and get a nice shot. We shake hands.

"Will you give me a copy?"

"Of course," I say. "I'll get one made for you in town tomorrow. Now I must get back to work. "*Proschai Yuruchka.*" Farewell, little Yura.

- - - - - - - - - - - - - - - - -

Tatiana Viktorovna, 49, is a reticent woman with a commanding air that projects strength of character as well as competence. She goes about her work with neither fuss nor drama. The children like and respect her.

We try to give the very best care to these children but it is not easy. The problem is that they are with us for such a short time, most of them only a few weeks. A year at the most. We try to increase their level of culture and to create a decent atmosphere. I think we have succeeded to a large extent but I am concerned about what happens to them after they leave us.

A dietskiy dom is probably best for our kids in most cases, all things considered. I've been to two of them to visit children who had been in our priut. They were doing well. Certainly they were no worse than they were with us. But the best solution for our kids would be adoption. I don't know about older children but I've known families who didn't have their own children and adopted babies. It was a success in most cases.

Kids who get adopted are the fortunate ones. They are blessed by God. I knew three such children. Two are now graduated from university and the third is still only fifteen but he's doing well. Two I know moved into an unusual arrangement, a family home created for them by relatives. And I know three children who were adopted by Swedish people. They are leading very good lives.

I am an engineer by profession. I graduated from a technical university. Then I got a good job. But suddenly, after years with a perfect record, I was fired because my company went through a hard time. The same thing has happened to a lot of people. I looked but I couldn't find anything else. I was devastated. I cried and cried. Then somehow I got into this kind of work, child care.

I went to an agency to find a job, not for myself but for my daughter who is a dental assistant. The agency gave me a lot of phone numbers for places that needed help. One was this priut. They needed a vospitatilnitsa, not a dental assistant. I am very happy to have found this. It is important work.

From personal experience I know the value of children. At first I couldn't have any of my own. Then—a miracle!—I had one child and then another. But my son had a serious illness when he was young. He is all right now, but because of his illness I know how precious he is. I am very interested in helping children. There is no more important work in the world.

But it is very difficult work. Our major lack here is psychotherapy. One psychologist is not enough. And our psychologist is not equipped to do therapy, only diagnosis.

Here is why I think the children need psychotherapy: Children can't seem to find themselves in this life. They are confused. They see no personal or vocational future. They need help to believe in themselves and in their own strengths. They are not prepared to cope with the world. Many of them don't even know how to play. They have had no experience with toys.

We have a good staff and it is large enough. What we need are more toys and sports equipment. We need to have more things for the children to do. We used to have social clubs here but we don't now. It would be good to have them again but to staff and equip them, we need money.

Our salaries are very low. Nobody can live on them. For me it's even worse than for the others. I have parents who are ill and I must take care of them. I don't have time to take a second job as most of us who work here must do.

The most difficult thing is that these children have no notion of home. Many of them just want to go back to the streets. They must have someone who needs them. The majority have mothers who don't even want them.

The mothers try to bring children up all by themselves with no money. Their children have never known proper care. If it is offered, they resist it. Most have not had contact with decent men. Their fathers beat them or they don't know who their fathers are. They don't know anything at all about men. This is a terrible lack both for the boys and for the girls.

They call home where their mother is. It doesn't matter if she is a bad or a good mother. The very word "mother" is magic to them. When I take a child to hospital and the doctor thinks I am the child's mother and calls me that in front of the child, the child is very pleased. I am, too. I am honored.

- - - - - - - - - - - - - - - - -

Natalia Nikolaevna, 50, is an earnest, energetic woman who gets things done. She likes to take walks with the children and to play games with them along the way. She especially enjoys taking children to cultural events. She is an intellectual, an artist and an actress as well. There is an old fashioned, almost pristine quality to her and a touch of the bohemian as well.

I came to work here August 1, 1997. It's the sort of work toward which I've always aimed. When I was a teenager, I kept a diary. In the September, 1967, entry, I wrote that I hoped someday to become a vospitatilnitsa in an orphanage.

I studied in a teacher training institute. I majored in psychology. But my mother died soon after I started. I needed to support myself. To make matters worse, I came down with an inner ear problem. It was impossible for me to stay in school and to hold a job at the same time. So I dropped out of school.

I got my first job as a teacher and then as an artist making propaganda posters for the Communist Party. I am not a Communist. It was just a job and a good one. I held onto it for years. And then I came here.

I've always been interested in culture. Throughout my career, I've acted in the theater part time. I was fortunate to find Almus. Friends told me about it.

The biggest problem here is lack of money. If we only had money we could organize the children's time in a much better way. I want the children to be exposed to Russian high culture. As a group, they don't seem to like anything but sports. But when I have one or two children alone with me, I find that I can generate higher interests. They appreciate theater although they prefer the movies. Sometimes they are reluctant to show an interest in decent things in front of their friends. It's not "cool."

Although money will give us a better program, I really believe that this kind of work should be done for love, not money. It is the work of ordinary human decency. I do not think it proper to receive a salary for kindness and warmth. It should be the uncorrupted labor of the soul. But this country is in a terrible economic crisis and people must somehow survive. Compromises must be made. There is no alternative but to insist on being paid.

If it were up to me, I would open a private shelter for maybe three or four children who would live there with me for a long time; fifteen to eighteen years. I have no children of my own. This would be my family.

How could Almus be better? For one thing, young children and teenagers should not be in the same group.

The key problem here is that children don't believe in kindness or warmth. I think the goal of our program is to create warmth. If even one child becomes more humane because of our efforts, I will consider that my life will not have been in vain.

Children today are very selfish. Our program should help them think about others.

- - - - - - - - - - - - - - - -

Vospitatel Alexander Viktorovich, 37, "Sasha," is a thoughtful, private man not given to overt expressions of feeling. But in his quiet way, he generates many projects of interest to children. He is respected by young people and often may be seen in earnest conversation with them or planting a tree, building a shelf, or playing chess.

My field is astronomy. I graduated from St. Petersburg University and after that, I worked for ten years in a radio technical institute as a programmer. I was a member of the Communist Party during that time.

In 1990, I became interested in finding some kind of

work with children, particularly for those of Communist Party members. I worked in a dietskiy dom for a while, one that was affiliated with the Party.

I was motivated by an interest in being helpful to others.

The dietskiy dom was for older children. It was there that I became acquainted with Makarich who was planning a family-model dietskiy dom, the project that later became Priut Almus.

I worked at Almus from its beginning in 1991. We had immediate problems with the government. We were not allowed to set it up as a long-term dietskiy dom. We were permitted only to organize a priut, a temporary shelter. It was a second choice but we took it. I continued my work as a radio programmer during this time.

In 1994 or 1995 I obtained a full time job here, a duel role as teacher and vospitatel.

I'll tell you my personal motive for wanting to work with children: I have two children of my own but during the years of perestroika my wife and I quarreled and eventually divorced. She was given custody of the children and went with them to Canada. I haven't seen them in two years. I figured that if I couldn't raise my own children, I could at least help raise those of others.

Frankly, I am not pleased with how Almus has developed. The problem is that the relationship between the children and the teachers is unnatural. It has not become the family we had hoped for. Now it is nothing more than an ordinary state boarding school where children stay only for a brief period of time. We originally intended that the teachers be more like real family members, not merely instructors.   But that unfortunately is not how it worked out.

If we had been permitted to keep the children longer, we might have been able to organize a genuinely helpful rehabilitation program for them.

But I do think that the fact that the children attend local schools is positive.   When they mix with normal families, they don't feel so much like orphans.   All of them have learning problems, though.   Their motivation for study is low.   That means that we vospitatilye must do much more than we would with children from normal homes.

The central concern in our program is with the formation of moral values in older children, ten to fifteen years of age.

As to my professional future, I want to continue as I am now.   I am taking a course in social pedagogy.   When I finish, I will be a qualified social teacher for rehabilitation—what you call a "social worker" in your country.   It is much like training to be a vospitatel.

I myself had a difficult childhood and can sympathize with these children.   My parents divorced just as I was finishing secondary school.   My relationship with both of them had always been stressful.   Now it is okay.   They are old and need my help and support.

Despite problems, I always had people to support me.   My grandmother was wonderful and I had good teachers and colleagues all along.   I didn't need a boarding school and there were no priutye in those days.   I doubt that I would have gone to one anyway.   I had enough good people who were close to me.

- - - - - - - - - - - - - - - -

Last night the kids held a discotheque in the playroom downstairs. It combined a Russian version of rock music with overflowing adolescent juices. The best of them did a fast, athletic step not unlike what may be seen in Russian folk dances. There appeared to be little influence from the black American tradition as in US rock and roll.

The party lasted well into the night.

Halfway through the dance, Anna Sergeevna dropped in again to see if she could help me interview more children. Before we began our work, she and I partook of tea and cookies with three vospitatilye who happened to be on duty. After washing the tea cups, the women set up a meeting between all the children and me to be held immediately despite the late hour—after nine in the evening. They announced ten minute intermission for the discotheque, hauled chairs to the upstairs playroom, ushered in the children and requested that they sit down and listen.

Anna Sergeevna chaired and translated. She told the children that they could ask me anything they wished. Questions came thick and fast about such matters as my age, my wife's name and, only half jokingly, whether I would please bring them all to America.

A vospitatilnitsa suggested that they might like to hear about my project with Haitian children. I read them a moving autobiographical piece written by a girl in a Haitian orphanage. Although normally they could identify easily with such a girl, they were tired and giddy, their attention quickly flagged ... and so it was time for the discotheque to resume.

- - - - - - - - - - - - - - - - -

Eight-year-old Mariana and seven-year-old Nadya are drawing brightly colored trees on the paper I brought back from the Vrachi Mira office. Mariana immediately wrote "To Bob" on hers. Then Nadinka did the same. They present them to me. I thank them and give each a kiss on the forehead.

The children gave me cookies the other night and last night Svetinka and Lyuba gave me neatly arranged twigs and green leaves in a jar of water.

Now Mariana and Nadya are playing games on the computer while sitting very close to me, a cozy moment. But they quickly lose interest in coziness and race out of the room.

Svetinka enters. She wants to play on the computer, too. I let her. Soon the room is packed with children yet again.

- - - - - - - - - - - - - - - - -

This morning Svetinka cried because someone took a safety pin of hers. Nadinka put her arms around her and told her not to cry. Eight-year-old Zhenya, who often provokes people by punching them, curled up next to Svetka and asked her why she was so sad. *What* a fine fellow! This Zhenya is a bundle of paradoxes.

- - - - - - - - - - - - - - - - -

I had more bread on my dinner plate than I was able to eat. I distributed the excess around the table, first to Zhenya on my right, then to Nadya on *his* right. I was planning to give the third piece to Anya, the cognitively handicapped girl who sat on *Nadya's* right. But before I could do so, Nadya herself passed the piece I had given her on to Anya.

Nadya is very protective of Anya.

We went for a walk. The kids held hands, not because they were told to but because that is their custom. Seven-year-old Nadinka is very popular. She could have been anyone's partner. But she chose Anya, the handicapped girl, and held her hand firmly the whole way there. But on the way back, nobody held hands. They all raced along instead in a mighty horde.

Zhenya pretends to grab food or whatever is edible and available—the crayons in my sitting room, for example. He announces himself as a Very Bad Boy. But when he is not being bad, he actually waits his turn and makes requests politely. Before coming into my room, he peeked in first and asked, "*Mozhno?*" May I?

An interview with Zhenya as translated by Anna Sergeevna:

> nya, Age 8. Zhenya is an active, sometimes
>   fellow who walks in a stiff-legged Russian male
>   He is a natural athlete and clown and thrives
>   n whether positive or negative. He is often

the first one in my room each morning and the last one to leave at night. He loves to have his picture taken and to pose making stupid faces.

I like Almus because the food here is great and I like the clothes they give you. The vospitatilye are good. And Sasha and Dima are my best friends.

The reason I'm here is that my mother doesn't like me. My home is no good. I ran away and the police took me to priut "Vera," and then Klavdia Aleksandrovna, the assistant director at Almus, met me there and brought me here.

My father used to beat me. That's why I didn't like it at home. My mother beat me, too.

I have three sisters, two of them are older and one who is little. One of them is in hospital now. I don't know why. Maybe she's sick. Another one is in a dietskiy dom and only one of them is home.

I like living at home but I don't like the people. My father likes me more than my mother does but he doesn't like me a lot. One of my sisters doesn't like me at all. I get along with the other two okay.

I cry a lot. I have nightmares, too, but not very often.

I want to go to a dietskiy dom after I leave here. That would be okay.

- - - - - - - - - - - - - - - - -

Jeff Groton, the American director of the Vrachi Mira office in St. Petersburg, told me that for the most part Russian families are gentle and loving. They tend to indulge children to a fault. This is an aspect of Russian culture I doubt most Americans are aware of.

Jeff explained that Russians tend to believe in the fundamental innocence of the child. They see children almost as a species apart, sort of like angels. They are tolerant of them and do not punish them even when they become difficult. They assume that it is just the way of the young.

The downside of this attitude is that it is hard to take angels seriously as full human beings.

Jeff was referring to the relative absence of battering punishments and sadism, not to such normal parental strategies as grounding which, I have come to understand, is common here in Almus and, for all I know, throughout all of Russia as well.

"But why, Jeff," I asked, "if children are indulged as you say do we so hear so many stories of sadistic, drunken beatings?"

"Russia is a country of phenomenal extremes," he explained. "There are many very, very good families. They actually represent the norm. But once you go outside the norm, it is like falling off a cliff. That's where to find the children we work with. There is no middle ground."

- - - - - - - - - - - - - - - -

I am in the dining room eating my fish cakes and mashed potatoes. Children shout *Priatnivo apetita!*—nice appetite—when they arrive—and *Spasibo!*—thank you—as they leave. There is constant talking and joking in between.

I am at Zhenya's table again. He has just served me the fish cakes. With a twinkle in his eye, he steals little Sasha's cup of tea and sets it down in front of me. I scold him and move it back to Sasha's place.

At another table, vospitatel Alexander Viktorovich—Sasha—is engaged in what appears to be a serious discussion with two teenage boys both of whom are named Andrei.

Lyuba, fourteen, Pasha, thirteen, and Alyona, twelve, are at one table, laughing together, talking girl talk.

Returning from the kitchen, Yura does a little dance while half-juggling his seconds of fish cakes.

There is a palpable dance-like rhythm pervading the room. It emanates from interactions among the children in the dining room, the epicenter of the jovial ambience. How much is due to the skill and commitment of the particular vospitatilnitsa on duty and how much to Almus culture? I can't say.

The place is well staffed.   Right now there are four vospitatilye on duty for some twenty kids. The evening shift will consist of two.

- - - - - - - - - - - - - - - -

Evening.   Another discotheque in the basement gymnasium.   Fortunately, I can't hear it in my room. However, after a while, curious, I wander down to check it out. Little kids and teenagers are jumping and kicking with those rapid, cake-mixer steps that the current Russian teenagers are so good at. But the pop music playing at the moment is, I am told, German.

Tolya is the disk jockey with the passionate—indeed volatile—help of Losha who a moment ago unceremoniously threw eight-year-old Zhenya out of the dance hall. I have no idea what Zhenya did to deserve this. Although I was looking in his direction at the time, I saw nothing but behavior identical to everyone else's, wild jumping around approximately to the music.

The vospitatilnitsa on duty also witnessed the expulsion but did nothing to intervene. Perhaps she saw justice in it. But maybe she finds Losha too intimidating to confront.

Zhenya is upstairs now, lonely, miserable, and staring at the flickering television set. I asked vospitatilnitsa Tatiana Viktorovna why he is there. "He doesn't want to go to the discotheque," she explained.

- - - - - - - - - - - - - - - -

Tolya, the disk jockey, tried to block the light coming in through the gymnasium windows by using wrestling mats and blankets. It is nine thirty on this St. Petersburg spring evening but there is still enough light outside to prevent the dance hall from feeling romantic. Twilight will stay on for almost the entire night.

Tolya was diagnosed by a psychiatrist as "schizophrenic." He had an explosive episode last year and was hospitalized for it. The doctor declared him mentally ill. Maybe but I don't see it. Although awkward socially, nothing about Tolya seems bizarre and, though odd, he seems to have social needs, contraindicative of schizophrenia. And he often finds himself a useful role in the group. He has taken charge of this evening's dance and has proven a tolerable disk jockey.

"He is fortunate," a vospitatilye said. "That diagnosis will get him good government benefits."

- - - - - - - - - - - - - - - -

Two of the children, Yura and the older Sveta, take razor blades to their lower arms and cut themselves until they bleed. Both have scars. I do not know if the staff does anything about this. I must ask a doctor.[6]

- - - - - - - - - - - - - - - -

Evening Tea Time. Vospitatilnitsa Natalia Nikolaevna knocked and, without waiting for a response, flung open the door to my room.

"Chai!" she announced. *"Tyi budish chai?"* Tea! Will you have tea? *"Konyechno,"* I answered. *"Budu. Chas."* Of course. I will. Just a minute.

Tatiana Viktorovna joined us in the staff kitchen next to my room. The doctor, a woman who works in the admissions clinic downstairs, came too as did Sergei, the student of computer technology. He is in charge of the Almus computer down the hall from the doctor.

"Kushat'!" Eat, Natalia Nikolaevna commanded, pointing to the cakes and cookies that wereartfully displayed on the table.

"Mamushka!" Little mother, I teased. She laughed. She is almost twenty years my junior.

"Ko sozhaleniiu, ya ne mogu poest." Unfortunately, I

---

6   Unfortunately, I never got around to doing it.

can't eat, I said. *"Khachu tol'ko nemnogo chai."* I only want a little tea.

Her face registers disapproval and concern for my health.

This scene repeats itself three times a day. At least.

- - - - - - - - - - - - - - - -

Another thing about Russians. They devour sweets. Yet there is pervasive concern for health in this country. The doctor on duty circulates daily among the children. She wears a white coat and carries a tray laden with vitamins. She hands them out, I note, only to some children. Why not to everyone? I have no idea. Maybe it is a matter of cost. Vitamins are probably expensive. If so, whom does she select, the malnourished or the healthy?

Vitamin supplements are balanced by an Almus diet heavy in starch and sugar and utterly devoid of fruits and vegetables, especially green ones. But meat often appears here in the form of cutlets of some kind or sardines that come fresh from the Gulf of Finland.

I've tried to do my part by buying fruit every time I return from center city. I brought home oranges the other day and today, apples. But interest in them is low. The oranges remained untouched in the staff refrigerator and I was the only person to take a slice of apple with my tea tonight.

- - - - - - - - - - - - - - - -

This morning when Natalia Nikolaevna, Tatiana Viktorovna and I had a pre-breakfast snack together in the vospitatilye kitchen, I passed orange slices around. The two women devoured these with relish. Natalia Nikolaevna smacked her lips. "They are delicious," she said. "I *love* oranges."

"But they are *so* expensive," Tatiana Viktorovna added. "We Russians can only afford apples."

A realization: People have not eaten the fruit I brought and left in the fridge for them because, oranges especially, are viewed as *treasures* properly belonging to me as owner. From now on I will personally invite each vospitatilnitsa to accept my orange slices, admonishing them that I will be insulted if they are not eaten at once.

I had not realized how phenomenally expensive everything in this country is for its citizens. At the same time, the market economy has made this a very *in*expensive country for those blessed to own dollars. The oranges I bought the other day cost less than a dollar a kilogram. But if one earns the equivalent of fifty dollars a month, a dollar is a whole lot of money.[7]

- - - - - - - - - - - - - - - -

Galina Mikhailovna, age 60. Galina Mikhailovna is a modest woman who tends to remain in the background. She enjoys her work and in her quiet steady way enjoys her work and is good at what she does. She generates expressive arts activities with the children and in a most maternal manner carefully attends to all their needs.

I finished school and entered a teacher-training institute. I grew up in a dietskiy dom. I was an orphan. (Tears

---

7   Since then the dollar has declined, and the ruble has increased in value

come to her eyes.)   For twenty-four years I worked in that orphanage. (She weeps softly.)

I found work here because I read in an advertisement that they needed teachers. That was when Almus was in the old place. I've been here five years. I liked it better when we were in the old location. It was more like family then. We brought up the little children as our own. It was a dietskiy dom but very informal and more like a real family.

We did many interesting things together.   Amazing things. The children visited Sweden, Finland and other places during their vacations.   Everyone says that Almus was much better then.

In those days, the children went to all sorts of after-school clubs. We also had a special teacher to prepare children for real life on the outside. The kids were taught to cook and to sew.

The main problem now is that the children are of a wide range of ages. The older ones are often negative. They smoke cigarettes and have other bad habits.

Makarich, our director, plans to divide the shelter into two units soon. One will be for younger children and one will be for the older ones. It will be better that way for both groups. We could help the older children really prepare for life with such an arrangement.

The other problem is a shortage of time. The children don't stay long enough. It is impossible to change habits in such a short period.

Another of Makarich's plans is to create a studio on the first floor. Some of the children are already taught to sew. That is a very good idea. They make batik under the direction of a professional artist who also teaches them to draw. But unfortunately there is a constant shortage of supplies and tools.

We would like to do more to help children create things with their own hands but there are never nearly enough materials.

We have a very friendly staff. We work together very well and try to make consistent demands on the children. I am responsible for nine of the smallest ones. Most of them go to school. But my attention has to be focused on those who stay at Almus. I try to be their teacher.

I think our kind of schedule—when we are here every three days or so—is the best way to organize ourselves. Almus is far from the center of the city and it is difficult to get here. If we had to be here every single day, we would get tired.

Almus is a very good place. All we need is more equipment. We lack toys. Children can't draw because there is no paper, no chalk; very, very little of everything.

I am already retired. This is my retirement job. I must keep working in order to survive. We can retire in Russia at fifty-five. But we get only a very tiny pension that isn't enough even to pay for an apartment.

Oh, it is terrible when you are no longer able to work! I don't like to think of what will happen to me. (She cries again.) I can't get help from my family. One of my two sons is unemployed. And my husband is unemployed, too. I don't like to think about these things. (She leaves the room in tears.)

- - - - - - - - - - - - - - - -

Irina Ivanovna, 55. Irina is a large woman who knows what she's doing. She has a direct manner that is firm but not antagonistic. She is concerned about the children as well as with the design and operation of the institution as a whole.

I got into this particular line of work because of the money. I've always worked with children, however. And I've always enjoyed it. My first job was as kindergarten teacher but it didn't pay enough. I looked around and happened to find Almus.

Four years ago I had no idea how to work with children like these. Almus was the first priut I've worked in and, as a matter of fact, this was the first time I even thought about the problems children such as these face. Now I think about their problems all the time. Even when I'm walking along the street, I think about the children, how they feel and how they live.

This place is good but there are ways to make it even better. We should have two units, one for the younger children and the other for the adolescents. Makarich is working on that. It does no good for the little ones to have the older ones around who are working out their adolescent problems.

It would be better if the vospitatilye worked every day in sequence so we could develop more stable relationships with the children and understand them more fully.

Take Losha, for example. He is very unstable. His behavior changes each day. We don't get to see the total picture. He is a very difficult child. When I'm here, he offers to protect the younger children from the older ones. But the next day he himself might suddenly take it into his head to beat them. The children are understandably frightened of him.

It's hard to function with the rapid changes in shift. But we work things out so that each of us is responsible for only two or three children. We are their counselors. We go to the neighborhood school with them and talk with the teachers and try to work with their parents. That brings a bit of consistency to what we do. But still, it's too bad that we can't be here every day.

This year we have Klavdia Aleksandrovna in a new role and that helps. She used to be a special teacher and now she is Director of the Second Floor, the residence director. As such she is here every day. Her job is to counsel the children and consult with the vospitatilye. She is very supportive and has an excellent mind. And she is in a position to follow the children closely during their stay with us. She is not regularly here on weekends but she sometimes does come in anyway if she is needed and, as a matter of fact, she sometimes sleeps here, too.

We do many good things with the children, particularly cultural things like taking them to museums or the theater. The children get in free everywhere in this country but unfortunately none of them are interested in high culture. The older ones only care about their disco dances and maybe in taking a walk now and then.

When this priut first opened, everyone thought it would be a long term residence for the children, a small, family style orphanage. But the government in its wisdom decided that we would only be allowed to provide short term care. The reason was that in St. Petersburg we were faced with so many street children that it was thought rapid turnaround would help us reach everyone. That was unfortunate reasoning. But what can you do?

When I first worked here, we had a good group of only five children and three workers. That was to have been our family. But the government decision turned all that around.

The keys to this place are the vospitatilye. Psychologists are not close enough to the real situation to understand what's going on. I've seen them try to get children back to their families but the families are often so terrible that it is not a good solution at all.

Vospitatilye must be serious, professional people who love children and understand their behavior and their needs. But more is involved than simply loving them, they must understand them.

- - - - - - - - - - - - - - - -

Tatiana Igor'ievna, 41. Tanya is a highly energetic person who works hard and smiles easily. She runs more often than she walks. Tanya is capable of having fun with the kids but she can also be businesslike if not stern. She has a good mind and sound judgment. The children like and respect her.

I worked in a kindergarten for 17 years before coming here. For the last three, I was the main child care worker. Each summer I took my children to a family summer camp where I also worked. The last year there, I was assigned to children who have special problems. I was the vospitatilnitsa for difficult boys between thirteen and sixteen years of age, thirty-six children in all. It was interesting work and I loved it.

I understood their problems and helped them in many ways. I cared for them and taught them. We got to really like each other and got along very well. We created a friendly, democratic atmosphere. I continued to help some of them in the city when they returned home. I talked with their parents and with their teachers and became involved with them on all levels. But in the winter, I went back to my job in the kindergarten.

Each year that I went back to the camp, I met different children. One summer I came to the conclusion that fourteen to sixteen-year-old girls are more difficult than adolescent boys. They are trickier and more complicated. If you tell a boy something, that's the end of it. With girls, it can go on and on forever. Girls require more individual attention.

After that summer, I met a women who said that she knew of a job for me here at Pruit Almus where I might work professionally with difficult children. Now I am really into it. I am going to university to become a certified vospitatilnitsa.

This is a very, very good place but we do have some problems. For example, it is impossible for the children to adjust to all the vospitatilye or for the vospitatilye to deal with all the children. Nobody with appropriately varied approaches can successfully handle that many different personalities. My own way is to listen. I have meetings with them once a week to give them an opportunity to discuss their problems. I think the others should do something like that, too.

Frankly, I don't think psychologists are much of a help.

If the vospitatilye notice that a child has a problem, they might refer him or her to the psychologist. The psychologist then works with the child but we notice that the problem continues just as it was.

Maybe if the psychologists discussed their findings with us, it would be useful. But generally they don't. Well, that's not entirely true. If a psychologist has time, she will briefly present the problems to us and we will talk about them. If she doesn't have the time, we hear nothing. I don't count on help coming from psychologists.

From the perspective of the child, there is no question: vospitatilye are more helpful than psychologists. There shouldn't be two professions in this work. There is really only one field—"People who Work with Children."

Another problem is that we don't teach children how to live in the real world. We used to do much more of that. We took trips to factories rather than just to museums and theaters. But for some reason we don't do it any more. We did have a meeting with the older girls once about professions. I remember Pasha explaining that she once studied dressmaking at school but then lost interest.

A huge problem is that we simply cannot live on our salaries. Most of us hold two or more jobs. We each have our own way of surviving. Take me for example. I have two children to raise. I have no husband. I go to school. I don't have time to take another job. Fortunately, my grandmother is able to help me a little.

Next year, after I've finished my studies, maybe things will get better.

- - - - - - - - - - - - - - - -

Little Sveta and I crashed into each other on the stairs while heading for the dining room. I offered her my hand. She clung to it. She desperately wants adult attention but can't seem to compete with other kids who manage to get to the grownups first. But thanks to this accidental meeting, she had me all to herself.

We danced down the stairs together.

As we were about to sweep into the dining room, she had me bend my head and in the tiniest whisper asked if I would please sit to her left at her table. But when she took her place in food line, Mariana slipped into her chair. Ignoring Sveta's timid protests, Mariana explained that she *really* had that seat first, *way* before we arrived.

Sveta shrugged, utterly defeated, with nothing to say in the face of Mariana's reasonable story.

Then the vospitatilnitsa on duty sat Sveta down opposite me instead of at my side where she wanted to be. But just as she was lowering herself into that second-choice chair, Dima appeared and announced that it was *his* place. "I called it first," he lied.

The vospitatilnitsa once again intervened. She said nothing to Dima but moved Sveta to an entirely different table. Sveta obediently carried her plate, glass and silverware and sat down at that far distant place without so much as a murmur of protest.

Later she rose to get seconds in tea. Losha immediately swept into her newest seat offering no justification at all. With a wave of his hand he dismissed whatever mild objections she might have offered.

Svetinka now had no seat at all. She finished her meal holding onto her plate while standing by the tea bowl. But toward the end of lunch as people were leaving, a space became available again right by my side. Sveta carried her food and silverware with her and sat down there, smiling her sweet, tiny smile.

Svetinka, age 8, is an engaging child with a sad face that reveals a longing to be cared for. She thrives on attention but is quickly put off by the slightest suggestion of rejection. If another child competes with her, she pulls into herself. She attracts bullies. But she recently seems to be making an effort to stand up for herself and has had some beginning success in doing so.

I live in Almus because my mother was drinking all the time so she sent me here. At home there is only my mother, my father and me. My father also drinks. He's done bad things but my mother never has. He never actually hurt me but sometimes he gets angry like once when I went walking alone and he didn't know where I was. He yelled at me. But when he isn't drunk, he defends me to other kids if they tease me. He gets mad a lot. My mom just sleeps when she is drunk.

When my father gets angry, I run and hide so he can't find me and hurt me. I hid in the closet once. He found me and beat me on the hands.

At first I didn't want to come here. But I like it now. Kids sometimes hurt new kids but then they become friends. That's what happened to me.

Here's what I like about Almus: I like the games. I like the stories the vospitatilye tell. I like living with a lot of children because at home I was alone. My best friends are Yulia, Mariana, Lyuba, Nadinka...and the other Nadya who is in the hospital right now.

After I leave, I will go back to my family if they come get me. I heard that when your turn is over here, parents have a half hour to get their children or they get sent to a dietskiy dom[8].

I cry sometimes. But I don't have nightmares.

- - - - - - - - - - - - - - - -

Mariana, 8, the one with the reasonable story, is a bubbly kid, interested in everything. She does well in school and is a constructive leader of the younger girls. But she shows signs of stress. Her lips are chapped because she sucks on them when tense.

I lived in another priut but I didn't like it there. It was boring. They didn't do anything. When my mother came to visit me, I told her how dull it was so she took me out and I came here.

It is really great here. I have a lot of friends. And my mother comes to visit me much more often than she could there. It's nearer to where we live. My sister, Sveta, is here, too. She was in the other priut, too, and hated it as much as I did.

We didn't like it there because the vospitatilye didn't take us for walks like they do here. The things that are good here are watching television, listening to music, reading books and playing futbol (soccer).

I am not living at home because we had a real bad housing problem. We lost our apartment.

8   Untrue

In my family, I have a mama, a papa, a grandfather, a grandmother, and my father has two brothers and seven sisters. My father, mother and grandmother lived with me and my sister in our apartment.

I am worried because I heard that my grandmother is sick and nobody knows where my grandfather is. Maybe he's dead. My mother doesn't know where he is either and his neighbors said that they haven't seen him for three days.

I miss home a lot but I like it here. The good thing about home is you can do what you want. Here there are rules. Like at home I eat anytime I'm hungry but here we have a time for breakfast, dinner and supper and here we have to ask if we want to turn on the TV or go for a walk.

- - - - - - - - - - - - - - - - -

Dimitri, age 9, looks as if he is on the verge of tears. He is an active boy but pulled into himself and marginal even to the freeform society of the younger boys. He is less mature and more dependent than the others in his age group.

I've been here a half year. I like Almus because it is good. I like to take walks and I've made a lot of friends. There's nothing I don't like about it here. How could this place be better? I think it could be but I don't know how.

I am here because my parents drink. They don't do anything bad when they drink. They just go to sleep.

I got sent here because my teacher and my grandma said I shouldn't live with my parents. I guess they were right. But I miss being home. I miss my family and my mother and my father and my friends and my grandmother. But they visit and I go home on weekends.

My mom and dad are working on their drinking problems. They are trying to stop drinking. No: I mean, they have really stopped already.

My dream is to go back home and live with my parents.

- - - - - - - - - - - - - - - - -

It is evening, past eleven. I've finished teatime with the vospitatilye. We gossiped about the children, those who are here now and those we remember from last year.

Because tomorrow is another vacation day and all the schools will be closed, another discotheque was held downstairs. There I was witness to the now familiar flashing lights and music that put ear drums at risk while each kid did his or her own special wiggle. Short boys danced with tall girls. And so on.

Losha danced alone, swinging his arms like a maniac, his feet spinning wildly.

Tolik was Disc-Jockey-in-Chief again, very much in charge but in his spare time he wrestled and giggled with the little children. He was gentle with them and almost humorous. I don't see mental illness here. Nothing but immaturity. Bizarre? Is he any more bizarre than the rest of them? They are all bizarre.

Tolik, age 16, is a tall, blond boy, handsome, intelligent and strong. He looks somewhat older than his sixteen years. But he desperately seeks attention and in that respect, he seems far younger. He may be observed galloping down the corridor with seven-year-olds, waving a toy pistol and shouting, *"bang-bang!"*

Beyond that, Tolik relates to others only marginally. He is alone much of the time. There is an ominous quality to him that is hard to define. That, I suspect, is what keeps age-mates at a distance. A vospitatilnitsa told me that a psychiatrist once diagnosed him as "schizophrenic." That may be accurate but I resist labels.

I've been here for more than a year and a half. I was sent because my father threw me out when my mother was in hospital. I'm glad to be out of the house. My father used to beat me all the time for no reason.

My mother is in a mental hospital. She was always a very nervous person but she never hit me. She was in hospital twice, the first time for only a few weeks. The second was for a very long time. She's been in there now for about seven months.

I have two brothers and three sisters. One of my brothers and two of my sisters are grown up and the others live with my father. When my mother first came out of the hospital, they all wanted to live with her but when she went back in the second time, they had no choice. They had to live with dad.

I go to school. It is a kind of institute for the trades. I study house painting and carpentry.

I think it's only so-so here. The best thing is that you can go to the movies alone and the worst thing is that they send you to bed too early. I have some friends here. Andrei is one.

If I do something wrong here, they don't really punish me. They just lecture me for a long, boring time. I irritate the vospitatilye. I don't know exactly what I do. But if I do something wrong and they give me a hard time, then I do something wrong on purpose just to get back at them.

When I grow up, I would like to get an apartment, a good job, and a wife and children. I want to work as a cook. I thought of being vospitatel myself once. I like kids.

I am here for such a long time because my mother went into the hospital just when I was ready to leave this place. I didn't want to go home to live with my father so they let me stay in Almus for more than a year.

- - - - - - - - - - - - - - - -

Consider Losha, the wild fourteen-year-old, charming, tricky as a monkey, sly as a fox, funny, angry, and a bully; often kindly and always manipulative. Mercurial. Losha can project a frightening aura, a foretaste of the fury that roars inside him. But his anger is also his form of theater that renders him at once titillating and scary. It maintains him on stage and at the same time places his audience at a distance that is safe for them as well as for him. From that position, he is able to manipulate people with more than usual skill. Children and adults alike find him entertaining but remain wary in his presence.

I've been here for four months. It's an okay place. But only so-so. It all depends on the vospitatilnitsa on duty. The bad ones don't give me enough freedom but the good ones give me food. The thing I like about it here is that it's a place to sleep and eat and there are people who will take care of my basic needs.

Each vospitatilnitsa has a different idea about what I should be doing. One makes me sit and do my homework all day. But another just says, "Do your homework." She doesn't push it. With her I can do what I want.

I am here because of family problems. My father—he's not really my father. He's my mother's boyfriend. He threw me out. He was always beating on my mother so I decided to beat the shit out of him. The son-of-a-bitch took a while to recuperate. After he got back on his feet, he threw me out.

That fucking bastard got himself another apartment where he took other women when he was supposed to be with my mother. So I went over there when he wasn't around and robbed him blind. I took everything I could find. Then the asshole tried to find me. He carried a gun to shoot me.

The problem is that my mother is a drunk and doesn't know how to take care of herself. She's been living with the creep for ten years, since I was six. He's been beating her and me that long. He doesn't touch me anymore, though. I am too big for him now. I can take him. But I have to protect my mother. I don't know why. She's completely out of it and she doesn't even like me.

Anyway, I was thrown out and lived on the streets for a while. It was cold out there and I wanted to get to some place where I could be in school. If you don't get an education, you don't get a profession. If you don't get a profession, you are a nobody. So I knew this friend who called some psychologist who brought me to Priut Vera and from there they sent me here.

My future? I want to be a baker someday. That's why I want to study.

I worry about my mother. The last time I went home, the shithead beat my mother again and he beat my brother and sister, too. They aren't my real brother and sister. They are his kids with my mother. My brother is nine and my sister is eleven.

So anyway, I went to the police. But they asked me to come back and bring my mother and the two kids but my mother was too scared to go. She thought the asshole would kill her if he found out. So I went anyway with my brother and sister.

The police sent the kids and me to a doctor. The doctor found a big scar on my brother's head. He asked him where he got it. Serogia, my brother, lied and said he fell.

Everybody knows about my family problems. The neighbors reported us to the police a lot of times. Nothing happens, though. All my mother does is drink. I don't know what to do. Last time I saw her, I told her she's got to see a doctor. I said if she didn't, she would never see me again.

I never knew my father. I don't know anything about him. All I know is that my mother says he is living somewhere in St. Petersburg.

I will kill my mother's boyfriend, that fucking asshole. I don't care what happens to me. I just want him dead. I will kill him.

When I grow up, if *I grow up, I have no idea what kind of life I will lead. I live from day to day now and probably always will.*

- - - - - - - - - - - - - - - -

This morning as I sat typing, Losha popped his head in at the door and asked if he could play computer games. "Not now, Loshka," I said. "But come on in anyway and sit down. Just be quiet. I must finish my work." He entered and sat still and silent. When I came to a good stopping place, I let him play on the computer for the next fifteen or twenty minutes and sat next to him and watched. He is quick and clever. There was a good feeling between us.

A crowd of noisy little boys barged in. The main characters were Zhenya, Sasha, and a couple of Dimas. They were in too wild a mood to trust with the computer. "Later, boys," I said. Then: "But you've got to get out for now. Out! Out!! See you guys *later.*"

Losha helped me get rid of them by ending his own game and closing the computer lid. He diplomatically urged the boys to get going by explaining, "Bob has work to do." Then he, too, left, smiling politely as he sauntered out the door.

Earlier, Irina Ivanovna and Tatiana Igor'ievna opined, "Someday that kid will end up either rich or in prison." It occurred to me that there might be another possibility. He might just become an ordinary person, a nice guy, a good citizen with a loving family and a useful job ... maybe in computer technology. Or child psychology. Who is to say?

- - - - - - - - - - - - - - - - -

Dr. Alla Pavlovna Surovteva warmth is always evident. So is her canny manner that pierces all defenses. She finds her way at once to the heart of any matter, discarding chaff with neither ambivalence nor regret. She is tough. But her manner of dealing with children is modest and respectful. She soothes and compliments as she firmly presses her views.

With Assiya there to translate, Alla asked how I thought mental health services might be offered here to better advantage. She said that she herself, a mere physician, knows nothing about psychology.

"In fact," I said, "you are a *great* psychologist."

"But I depend on you to tell me what to do," she said. "My goal," she added, "is to bring the mental health services here up to the standards of the West."

"The standards of the West are dreary," I said. "Far too much attention is given there to the self."

"Under the Communists there was no 'self' at all," she said. "There was only, 'The People.'"

"We need then to come up with something better than what either the West or the East has offered thus far," I suggested.

"The way I see it," I continued, "is that the child lives in a context comprising biology, family, friends, school, the economy, the community, the nation; indeed the entire world. If we see the child as an isolated entity, we miss much useful information and we set unnecessary limits to intervention possibilities.

"If we focus our efforts solely on psychotherapy, we see—or *think* we see—only what may be within the particular psyche of the given individual. But if we take as our object of concern not the particular person alone but his or her entire multifaceted context as well, we give ourselves an opportunity to view, and hopefully to accomplish, considerably more.

"Before working with an Almus resident, we might first consider the societal or institutional factors here that could mitigate against his or her healthy development. One of these might be the simple matter of the staff rotation schedule. With a new team on duty every day and the consequent changing rules and expectations, it might be difficult for a child to acclimate and stabilize, especially if that child comes from a chaotic home as most of them do.   Worse, how under such fluid circumstances is a child to form attachments to any of the available adults?

"And, with daily changes, it is well neigh impossible for the vospitatilye to generate programs that grow and mature on a daily basis.

"It seems to me that a key mental health agenda item in priutye," I concluded, "should be to create a context in which relationships are stable, attachment is facilitated and sound programs may evolve and develop.

"To create such a context, we need to focus on vospitatilye and children as a unit. Vospitatilye are the ones who deal with the children daily. While the child is in the priut, vospitatilye stand in for parents. If children trust them, they will look up to them, turn to them for direction and work through their most personal thoughts and issues with them.

"Friends may be even more important. Children exert an enormous influence on one another. Conversations with friends are generally of greater import than anything that might transpire with adults. It is unfortunate that there is such a constant and rapid turnover of children here. But it can't be helped and might even be an advantage in that it militates against institutionalization and maintains the priut as a flexible resource, available to everyone in the community as the need arises.

"Were I to work here as a psychologist," I went on, "I would invent a broad, hard-to-define role specific to me rather than accept being somebody else's vision of a psycho-diagnostician or psychotherapist. I would learn about the children through observation and play. I would then try to become a sounding board for the vospitatilye and the children themselves.

"What I am describing is a kind of fluid, informal, conversational approach consistent with my training and inclinations. It would permit me broad, institutional impact and, incidentally, would be far more interesting personally than sitting in an office administering tests or in dogged exchange with one child at a time every fifty minutes.

"Finally, I wonder why *anybody* would waste time with psychodiagnostics? Why bother with an elaborate exposition of the problem if the reality is that one treatment fits all? In medicine, it is important to know if the patient has tuberculosis or a broken leg because there are distinct treatments available for each.

"The field of mental health is otherwise. What *difference* does it make if a child is neurotic or depressed? In either case we prescribe the same things: a stable, optimistic environment, conviviality, adults who listen, an opportunity to learn, and a healthy peer group."

Alla listened carefully.

"What you are describing," she said, "is a way of working that leads each caretaker to function according to his or her own lights and for each child to be viewed as an unique individual. That is a new way of thinking for us post-Soviet Russians although it was common long ago. Under the Communists, the goal was for everyone to be the same. It has only been within the past eight years that some of us have begun to consider other possibilities. There have been many changes recently in our country but we obviously need to go further. You are describing a synthesis of *obschinost and lichnost,* but neither one nor the other. Interesting."

- - - - - - - - - - - - - - - -

At long last, this was to be my first in-depth conversation with Mikhail Makarievich, the founder and director of Almus. Alla Pavlovna joined the conversation as did Jeff Groton, American director of the US-sponsored office of Doctors of the World, "Vrachi Mira," in St. Petersburg. Jeff also translated.

Makarich is a visionary who has devoted himself heart and soul to raising children who do not have functioning families. He himself was raised in a dietskiy dom and experienced first hand the sterility of traditional Russian institutions where children are essentially inmates, incarcerated and isolated from normal life. His vision is the creation of a non-institution, a surrogate family that cares for a very small number of children at a time. That was his original design for Almus but forces beyond his control caused it to grow into something far larger although still tiny by the measure of traditional institutions.

Makarich regrets the loss of his original dream but is pleased with the success of what he has achieved. His intention remains for Almus to be a democratic oasis where children are respected and learn to cope successfully with life beyond the walls of the institution. Almus is indeed all of that. But Makarich continues to strive for even more.

He is restless.   He speaks passionately and at considerable length while waving his arms up and down for emphasis in great, sweeping gestures. Makarich has a kindly face, mischievous eyes, a bald head and a black mustache. He is in his late forties. Although engaging, he is also intense, driven, but surprisingly hard to discern. A private passion about which I have no clue seems to drive him.

Makarich was already acquainted with some of my views. He read most of my translated notes from last year and said that he likes them.

Together, we considered what an ideal role for a psychologist might be in an institution such as Almus. He and I agree in seeing the psychologist as a person who seeks an overview of both the child and his or her entire context—the family, the community and the institution. With such a perspective he or she would be in a position to contribute on a program level.

We agree that the psychologist should observe and provide feedback to staff and children alike. But he or she should not be in a separated or elevated category. Care taking roles should overlap freely, merge and be played out according to the capacity of the players and the needs of the children. The only difference between a psychologist and a vospitatilnitsa is that the former is positioned to have an overview of the child in context whereas the latter works with the child on a day to day basis. But both parties would participate in planning and both would have contact with the children

"A psychologist," I said, "should be like a man of the theater as you are, Makarich, or a grandparent as I try to be. He or she should concentrate on general issues such as morale and ambience and on setting the scene. Once that scene is set, the children take over and improvisation proceeds apace."

This was a good first meeting. I hope we have more. We are thinking along similar lines.

- - - - - - - - - - - - - - - - -

Natalia Nikolaevna, vospitatilnitsa, took a group of six younger children for a walk. I went with them, offering shoulder rides and free photographs to anybody who asked. We came to a nearby playground where the children climbed, jumped and whirled on all the equipment.

Yura stood to the side, puffing on a cigarette without any effort to conceal his transgression of policy. He asked me to take a picture of him like that, smoke swirling around his head.

"Don't you try to stop little children from smoking?" I asked Natalia Nikolaevna.

"There's not much we can do about it," she confessed with a shrug. "The children are here for a short time and bring the bad habits of bad families and bad streets with them. We have too many other things to worry about."

- - - - - - - - - - - - - - - -

Yura, 10.   Yura is a towheaded street urchin whom Chaplin would have done well to cast as The Kid.   He walks with the signature swagger of Russia men.   He is combative and blows up quickly.   When people give him what he considers a hard time, he bursts into angry tears or he swings his fists wildly and powerfully.   But he responds to adult affection and kindness which transform him as if by magic into a sweet little boy. Almost.

It's okay here but the vospitatilye are afraid that kids might escape so they don't let us go far.   The big problem is that you can't get cigarettes here. They let you smoke which is okay but you ask the vospitatilye for cigarettes and they don't give you any.   So we beg them from people in the streets or pick up butts from the sidewalk.

I was three when I started smoking.

I've been here a week.   I came because my mother drinks.   I don't have a father but I have a little brother who is a year and two months old.   When my mother gets angry, she hits and she can really hurt.   She beat me real bad many times.   She doesn't say why she beats me except she yells things like, "Fuck off!"

I ran away from home and slept on a factory floor.   They found me and brought me here.   It's not as good here as it would be if they gave you cigarettes.

I do okay in school.   When I grow up I want to be an

astronaut. I know they don't let astronauts smoke because in zero gravity cigarettes will fly around. So I will stop someday. But that won't be for a while.

I hate hard alcohol. I wouldn't ever drink anything but beer.

I wish they let you sleep late here. That and no cigarettes are the worst things about this place.

But the good thing is they give you medical help. I get headaches real bad.

- - - - - - - - - - - - - - - - -

At dinner last night Alyona walked straight to Yura's table and engaged him in earnest conversation.

"What could those two *possibly* have to say to each other?" I wondered. "There are worlds of difference between them. She is a sophisticated twelve-year-old and he's a ten-year-old urchin." The answer soon became evident. I noticed him slip her a cigarette and she slipped him something in return. Hard cash, I guessed.

A few minutes later thirteen-year-old Pasha approached the same Yura. A similar transaction took place.

Pasha caught my eye as she returned to her seat. I shook my head, "*Nyet, Nyet, Nyet,*" I mimed in disapproval of the deal I was certain she had pulled off. She smiled sheepishly and shrugged her shoulders as if to say, "That's the way it is."

"Tell me, Pashinka, how much do you pay for each cigarette?" I asked.

"Two rubles," she said.

A couple of vospitatilye had been on duty. Either they didn't notice or they didn't care.

- - - - - - - - - - - - - - - - -

Dinner. Losha said something loud, absurd and, I imagine, obscene to the little children at his table. I could not understand any of his words but I picked up his savage tone.

The younger children are attracted to Losha because he is amusing. But at the same time, they keep their distance. He can also be scary. But seven-year-old Nadinka knows how to handle him. She looked him right in the eye and twirled her index finger on her temple to express her opinion on the state of his mental health. Then she collapsed into giggles.

In his best English, not a word of which Nadya understood, Losha barked, "Mother-fucking-shit-eating-whore-bitch!" after which he giggled, too, but evilly. I think he respects her in his own way.

Then Svetinka, emerging from the victim mode, pretended to stab Losha with his own fork, tittering all the while. He took it well. He grabbed his fork back and play-wrestled with her. She thought the whole episode hilarious. Losha is great fun.

- - - - - - - - - - - - - - - - -

Three little girls, Nadya, Sveta and little Lyuba, wandered over to the neighborhood school which is no more than a hundred yards away from the priut. I followed. They wanted to play hopscotch on the patio in front of the entrance. Losha spotted us and came whizzing up on Almus roller blades. The girls teased him, giggling. They ran up, poked him and danced away. In a flash he whooshed around and roared full speed at them, scooped them up, raced away with all three over his shoulders and then dropped them off again further down the court. The girls squealed with delight.

Losha was in his fun-loving, big brother mode, titillating but not dangerous. The anger he harbors was transformed into horsing-around energy.

Losha knows that I see something positive in his wild games. He screeched to a stop beside me.

"Bob," he ordered. "Give me two rubles for cigarettes!"

"Forget it," I said. "Smoking is bad for your health."

"So? *Ice cream, then!* Ice cream, ice cream! Buy me *ice cream!* I *love* ice cream. I *need* ice cream! I *must* have ice cream!" He put on a pouting baby face.

I bought ice cream for them all and told the girls to thank Losha. "He made me do it," I said.

- - - - - - - - - - - - - - - - -

Just before bedtime, Losha stomped into my room. He asked to play computer games but I was busy writing so he made himself at home. He sat politely, hands folded, content.

Then: "Your dictionary of Russian slang!" he commanded. "I *must* see it!"

He spent the next half hour convulsed over English

equivalents of Russian slang words and phrases. *"Eat shit!"* he yelled. *"Motherfucker!"* he screamed.

I was embarrassed. I had purchased the dictionary in New York. Barnes and Noble, a legitimate source. But I had only flipped through it, never having read it closely. Too late now.

Arkesh had the good fortune to visit at that point. The boys cracked up together. When Arkesh finally departed, the older Andrei arrived and the hilarity continued. Andrei, too, wandered off eventually and sixteen-year-old Sveta dropped by hoping for her turn on the computer. But she had no interest in obscenities.

"Losha is crazy," she confided.

Losha asked to borrow the book until tomorrow. He promised to return it. "Sure, Losha," I said.

- - - - - - - - - - - - - - - -

Some days later: I wonder if Losha will ever return my slang dictionary. I asked him for it a while ago. "It is in my room," he said. "I'm still reading it." I wouldn't have minded donating it to him. It's a perfect present for him. I am as charitable as the next guy. But I cannot abide thievery.

- - - - - - - - - - - - - - - -

Sveta, age 16. Sveta looks like an adult and behaves like one. When I first met her, I thought she was a new staff member. She is good-natured and cooperative. But she seems more like a boarding house resident than a member of the adolescent peer group.

I've been here a year. I like it very much. I feel secure because I am on an independent living plan. I lived for a while with a friend in an apartment but the friend left. Being alone, I found it hard to manage. But here I can come and go as I please and I can be also be taken care of. During the day I go to school. I am a first year secretarial student. It is a four year course. I have three more to go.

I like everything about Almus, especially the way it's managed. I really like the vospitatilye. The demands are different for the younger and older children. I am the oldest kid here. I like all my relationships with the children and the staff.

My dream is some day to have my own room with a phone, a TV set and a computer. I know it sounds like a fantasy. But I think it will happen.

You see, I hope to get my grandmother's old room in her kommunalka, *her communal apartment. My grandma died but she didn't leave a will. I am the only one of her relatives who needs the space. The case is now being decided in court. If I win, I could live in that room and continue my studies. I think I will win.*

I won't have a family of my own for at least ten years so I can finish preparing for a career. I want a good career so I can have money to raise my children in case my husband leaves me. I want a husband I can trust. We will have children together. I'd like to travel, too.

I don't want my children to go through what I did. When I was little, I lived at home with my mother and father. When I was about six years old, my father left us. Then my mother found a boyfriend and he insisted on selling our apartment. That's when I went to live with my grandmother. She had this room in the kommunalka.

My mother just sort of wandered around. She didn't worry about me so I didn't worry about her. My mom got depressed and started drinking around this time. I was about thirteen.

I loved my grandmother. I tried to take care of her. She was very old. I went shopping for her and did all the cooking. Then she went to the hospital. I visited her there. And then all of a sudden my mother appeared in my life again. But at that same time, my grandmother died.

My mom said she would bury grandma. But she just disappeared again and I was left alone once more. I had to bury my grandmother by myself.

I went to live with a girlfriend and while there, I heard about this priut. I was lucky that they took me in.

As for my father: I see him often now. He is a real alcoholic. He lives with his brother and his mother. I go there to visit her, not him. This grandmother is also a very nice person. She doesn't drink or smoke and she supports her two sons on her tiny pension.

I visit her because I miss her and I really love her. I see my father when I am over there but we hardly ever talk to each other. I don't want to help him because he didn't pay attention to me for all those years when I was growing up.

I don't have a boyfriend and I don't want one. I have other things to do with my time. Boys don't give you a chance to study.

For my future, I just want my troubles to be over and to lead a normal, secure life.

Almus is almost perfect. Everybody here feels like brothers and sisters. I think they should make this place bigger. But I guess more kids could create a problem. Maybe they should open a lot more places like this.

The best thing about Almus is that they don't make you study but they explain that you should or your life will be terrible.

But it's hard for me to find real friends here, people I can really talk to. The kids seem much younger than me.

- - - - - - - - - - - - - - - -

Quite the opposite of Sveta is Lyuba, age 15, a tall, angular girl, athletic and an excellent dancer. She sticks up for her friends, the two other teenage girls currently living in the priut. Lyuba is a classic Western adolescent rebel. She fusses with makeup in any mirror she can find and flirts aggressively with the boys. There is also a hardness to her, a shell, a remoteness that makes her difficult to know. Lyuba's top incisor teeth are missing, a major disfigurement for someone so concerned with how she looks.

My parents beat me. They drink and go crazy and throw me out of the house. It went on and on like that. I couldn't stand it. Sometimes I would run away and sometimes they made me leave.

They began beating me when I was about thirteen. They couldn't control me. I would come home late and I wouldn't help around the house. But it was only when they got drunk that they would beat me. I have two younger brothers and two older sisters. They don't get beaten. It was only me. I don't know why.

I've been in Almus for three months. I was in Priut Vera before that. I liked Vera all right. But I like this place better. This priut is much quieter. I like it quiet. And I like the vospitatilye here. They are very cool. I really like the kids, too. I have a lot of friends. They are all great kids.

The reason I like the vospitatilye is they don't yell at you.

My hobby is getting my body in shape. I go to an exercise gym. I love to dance. My favorite sport is running and also figure skating. In the winter, I go figure skating all by myself and all year long I go to the gym every day. I am an average student.

When I grow up, I want to have a good life, two children, a decent husband, and a happy marriage where we don't fight. I'd like to have enough money for food. We definitely won't drink.

Drinking is awful. I don't want a husband who drinks. I don't drink and I never will.

My front teeth got knocked out in a stupid fight over which was our favorite music group. Somebody whacked me with a stick. I'm going to get false teeth soon so I won't look so bad. When it's time to leave here, I won't go home. I'll tell the vospitatilye that I want to go to a dietskiy dom.

It will never work out at home as long as my parents drink. There are some counselors trying to help my parents get over their drinking problem. But it won't work. Nobody can help them. It's too bad. I feel sorry for them. They drink too much.

- - - - - - - - - - - - - - - - -

I enjoy taking photographs of children and distributing prints to them as soon afterwards as possible. I never tell kids to smile but they often do. Their faces often take on a radiant, thoughtful cast, sometimes moody, sometimes concerned.

The prints are popular. The children put them away in special places or give them to special people, family members, boyfriends, girlfriends, or vospitatilye.

Svetinka said excitedly, "You took *three* photographs of *me* already!" She showed me the album in which she had carefully placed them.

Nadinka gave hers to vospitatilnitsa, Maria Vasilevna, who said, "Oh, thank you, Nadinka!" and then arranged the picture in a prominent place on her desk.

- - - - - - - - - - - - - - - - -

We went for a walk. Anya was part of the group. Anya has what I believe is a genetic anomaly consisting of a small head, odd but pleasant facial features, musical talent, and a mild cognitive disability. It is not Fetal Alcohol Syndrome but I suspect that Anya might have Williams Syndrome[9] instead, something I read about and saw some years ago in a television broadcast of neurologist Oliver Sacks' work.[10]

---

9   http://www.williams-syndrome.org

10 http://www.oliversacks.com/films.htm

Anya asked me again and again and again to take pictures of her as she posed, smiling prettily.   A week ago she was camera shy but she has become increasingly committed to the picture-taking routine. Now she is eager, indeed she demands, to have her picture taken.

My policy: A copy of each photograph of an individual is given to that person. Photographs with two or more people in it are given to Priut Almus for putting on the wall or to be placed in the community album.

Photographs, carefully taken, are a way of acknowledging a child and making him or her aware not only *that* they are seen but *how* they are seen. It breaks through their sense, common in this population, of inadequacy, the belief that they are ugly or, worse, invisible. It is a rare child in Almus who feels beautiful. A beautiful portrait may open the door to a better sense of self.

- - - - - - - - - - - - - - - - -

One of the first words I learned in this country was *"morozhenoye,"* ice cream. It is a popular treat here, surprising in view of the very cold climate. I bought ice cream—watery Russian popsicles—this afternoon for the whole Almus gang, vospitatilye included, and distributed them after dinner with considerable fanfare. There was no particular reason for this other than impulse and high spirits. Yura demanded his after the party was over even though he had long since eaten his share. "But you didn't give me my *ice cream*," he whined. Bent on vengeance when I contradicted him, he tried to rummage through things in my room.

He went so far as to put his grimy fingers on my new used

camera. In a fury, I threw him out. I felt like punching the little snot. But I managed to restrain myself—barely. I wish I were like those remarkable vospitatilye, even of keel, stedfast and invariably pleasant.

- - - - - - - - - - - - - - - -

I sit here alone, typing. Alyona and Pasha knock on the door and march in, hauling mop and bucket with them. "May we clean your room?" they ask. But of course! *Konyechno*! I sneak extra ice cream to them as a special *spasibo*—thank you—for the offer and give each a peck on the cheek.

Some kids here are difficult. But most are marvelous. This is also true of most who are also difficult.

- - - - - - - - - - - - - - - -

At breakfast, vospitatilnitsa Irina Ivanovna, sits at the table like the captain of a great ship, arms spread like wings, commanding, interrogating, cajoling each and every child. Her manner is calm. She projects strength, mastery, and full confidence that her instructions will be followed.

"Have you eaten enough?" she says to one. "You have cereal left in your bowl," she observes to another. "Please see that your bed is made," a third is told. "Go upstairs and clean up your room!" she instructs a fourth. The children do as they are told. She doesn't threaten and they don't argue.

Those so designated line up for vitamins. Zhenya waits with an open hand. The doctor, in her professional white smock, gravely places four pills, two yellow and two red, in his open palm. "*Spasibo*," Zhenya says.

The doctor hugs him.

Nadinka skips out the dining room door. "*Priatnivo apitito!*" she shouts to all who remain.   Eat well! "*Spasibo!*" she yells to the cook.

- - - - - - - - - - - - - - - - -

Another vospitatilnitsa was in charge of the dining room at yesterday's breakfast along with another doctor. Tomorrow there will be yet another team.   The very same scene plays itself out again and again regardless of the cast of characters.   Is this a holdover from the Communist notion that order is valued over spontaneity, that people are interchangeable and that an emotional attachment to particular people is bourgeois nonsense? I do not know. I babble.

All the grownups evidently know these children well and feel, if not exactly maternal love for them, at least generous commitment. That is no small thing.

Why do we in the States imagine that a child requires no more than one or two parents or parent surrogates? So *what* if there are a dozen mothers? If it is good to have a mother isn't it better to have a dozen? The same surely applies to fathers. And grandparents.

Is a sense of one-on-one ownership, parent-to-offspring, requisite for proper development? Who knows? We humans may be hard-wired for that. Yet, looking around this priut, I am inclined to believe that we are more likely designed to be part of a grand family with siblings, aunts, uncles, grandparents, and a handful of parents thrown in for raucous good measure.

- - - - - - - - - - - - - - - - -

One of the two older Svetlanas—Mariana's big half-sister—left Almus for good last night. Her mother came to fetch her. I took farewell photographs of the family, then a portrait of Sveta with her mother, another with Mariana alone and then one with Sveta surrounded by the Almus boys she likes best, Losha and Arkesha.

"Why are you going, Svetka?" I asked.

"I don't like it here," she said. "I want to go home."

Odd. She *acts* as if she likes it here. She always *seems* happy.

- - - - - - - - - - - - - - - - -

Svetlana, age 14. Sveta is a warm, active girl. Highly social, she gets along with everyone. The older boys are attracted to her, an interest that is probably reciprocal. But on the surface she appears indifferent. Although she presents herself as easygoing, she is a rather tense person. Sveta has scars on her left forearm where she is in the habit of cutting herself. Her little half-sister, Mariana, lives at the priut, too. Mariana bites her lips so much that they are always chapped.

The reason I'm here is that the government said that our house uninhabitable. It was a nice house in a way because it is only two stories tall but it was very old and the wallpaper had mostly fallen off. The walls were always wet. Mushrooms grew right on the floor. It was definitely unhealthy to live there.

The city offered us another apartment. We took them up on it but they still haven't found us one. The police came and said that us kids had to live in a priut for a while. First, my sister and I went to a place called "Detei v' Opostnosti" (Children at Risk). We hated it there so our behavior wasn't very good. So, we got thrown out and they sent us here.

What we did there was mostly to use bad words. Well, we also fought with the other kids and we didn't go to bed when we were supposed to. Mariana took a stamp and a stamp pad and printed silly things all over everything in the bathroom.

The kids there were really boring. They were too goody-goody. The vospitatilye had them intimidated.

But I really like Almus. We have much more freedom here. We can walk around outside and we get to go places like the circus and the movies. We also get to go to school right in our own neighborhood. Over there I had to wait for some kind of government approval to go to school. Here, they sent me to one right away. And here you can even get help with your school work. I myself am not a very good student but I'm not too bad either. Mariana, my little sister, is great at school.

It's really better here than at home. At home it can get boring. Here you can hang out with your friends all the time. At home you're alone especially in bad weather or when you are sick.

Frankly, I don't like all the vospitatilye. Some of them flatter you at first to get information. Then they use it against you. When something goes wrong, they tell everybody!

At home I have a step father, my mama, and my grandfather. My real father is somewhere in the Far East. We used to live out there. Then my parents got divorced and we came to St. Petersburg. He stayed in the East.

My mother is very nice. She is a hairdresser and my stepfather is a long-distance truck driver. They get along with each other pretty well.

Here are my hobbies: I like to take walks. And I collect photographs and posters of Leonardo DiCaprio.

I am studying to be a hairdresser and to make clothes. I just started getting into clothes. When I was little, I sewed for my dolls at home.

Here are my suggestions for making Almus even better: One, separate the little kids out. Two, let us bigger kids take walks alone more. Three, let us go to bed at eleven, not ten. Ten is much too early for teenagers. Four, it is hard to have to deal with new vospitatilye every day. They each go by different rules. One day they told me I could sleep in the room I wanted to and the next day they told me I couldn't.

I cut my arms because I had an unhappy love affair. Other kids do it out of habit.

My favorite vospitatilye are Natalia Borisovna and Tatiana Viktorovna. Natalia Borisovna is a great person; and she's very smart. She knows how to organize neat games and she's got a great sense of humor.

Tatiana Viktorovna is nice, too, and she has a great sense of humor.

If I have personal problems, I talk with my friends.

There are two psychologists here who are okay; but I'd rather talk to friends. I don't think I'd ever talk to a psychologist—what would I do that for? But sometimes I do talk to the vospitatilye. It doesn't matter that much which one. If I had to, I'd talk to whomever happened to be on duty.

- - - - - - - - - - - - - - - -

Natalia Borisovna, 30. Natalia Borisovna works at close range to the children, particularly the older girls. She often sits in their rooms with them and they talk together late into the night. Kids crowd around her in the staff office or kitchen. She is like a big sister. Unlike other staff members who make their demands known to the children, firmly and unambiguously. Natalia Borisovna is more likely to reason and cajole.

I came here originally to do an internship in social pedagogy—social work—while I was a student at the Institute. Now I am working on a dissertation for the Candidate of Sciences degree.

I was hired four years ago and just stayed on. I love it here. I first tried working in a dietskiy dom to see what that was like but I hated it and got out of there right away. The atmosphere was oppressive and the anger generated within the children was hard to deal with. The problem was that the staff tried to make all children do the same thing. They didn't offer choices. Everybody had to participate. It didn't matter if it was going to the theater, playing games or watching television.

It is like a family here. The best thing is the way people deal with each other, adults with children, adults with the administration, and children with each other. I think the relationship between the children and the director is particularly refreshing and human.

Children here are not limited in what they can do. They have freedom within the limits of the schedule. They have real choices. They can learn new things.

My experiences here have influenced my thinking about the field. The staff is very dedicated. We study the theory and practice of work with children among ourselves. It's not organized for us. It's up to us. When we read an article that's interesting, we pass it around and talk about it when we get together over tea or whatever.

I try to practice new methods of communicating with children. I verbalize feelings. When a child cries or seems sad, I put words to what comes across to me. I give lectures on this topic now at the Pedagogical Institute.

I have a second job to make ends meet. Working here involves the organization of leisure time, the play activities of children, concerts and games: everything, even survival.

My main focus is to work with teenage girls who are particularly difficult. I try to learn their interests. I try to get close to them, to listen to them. They must have confidence in me if I am to play a role in correcting their behavior.

Every child here has his or her own psychological issues. We get to hear about them and try to help. And we also act as a liaison to the psychologists. The children often speak about their problems to us in a very open way.

The difference between the work of psychologists and what we do is this: Psychologists work with the "soul" of the child. We deal with all the other things, particularly behavior. Our concerns are practical. To tell you the truth, we don't always find that the psychologists have that much to offer.

It would be good if there were more and better communication between psychologists and vospitatilye. An exchange of opinions with them might be helpful to us and we might be useful to them in arriving at a correct diagnosis.

- - - - - - - - - - - - - - - - -

Tonight Makarich is going to take me to the annual spring opening of the drawbridges across the River Neva. It is the start of the prolonged national holiday that starts with May Day now seen as the exclusive province of diehard Communists and ends with the May 9 commemoration of victory over the Nazis. Victory Day is celebrated by everyone, Communists and everybody else. The opening of the bridges ceremony seems to be related to that holiday if only because of the coincidence of dates and the sense of renewal.

During the ice-free open water season from early May though late November, the bridges are raised each night from two in the morning until 5AM. This is to allow large ships to get in and out of the St. Petersburg harbor.

Before we left on our adventure, Makarich and I had a conversation over tea. Despite the absence of a translator, we communicated reasonably well. He is a theater person, a set designer, director and actor in a well-known children's theater group. He certainly has a theatrical manner, expansive and intense, full of energy, both of the nervous and the creative variety. He moves his hands up and down as he speaks even as we drink tea together. He swings them in great circles to create invisible images that may best be seen in his mind's eye.

Makarich has a shiny bald pate set in a crown of unruly black hair. A wiry, energetic man, when he stands it is with his feet squarely planted in place while his upper body, like that of a marionette, sways, bows and rises to the rhythm of his urgent speech. He speaks as if on stage, as if declaiming passionate verse. At least twice during our conversation, he broke into a Pushkin poem.

Makarich resides naturally in literature and the imagination. He is an artist; a fanatic but of a democratic sort. His effect on children must be entrancing. But, surprisingly I have seen him with them only rarely.

"Why," I asked, "is there no theater program for the children at Almus?"

The unfortunate language barrier prevented my fully grasping his answer. My sense, however, is that while he would like to institute such a program, there are numerous practical considerations that preclude it. One of these, if I understood him correctly, is that the children are not sufficiently talented.

(That can't be right!)

I must interview him again ... next time with a translator and a recording device.

- - - - - - - - - - - - - - - - -

Makarich and I plowed through the darkened city in Almus' ancient green Volga, a rickety, Russian-made, Jeep-like vehicle. Oleg, the chauffeur, was at the wheel. Serogia, the computer expert, came along at Makarich's insistence to serve as a translator. Serogia has taken some courses in technical English. His command of the spoken language is better than my Russian—but not by a whole lot. Nonetheless, we all managed amazingly well.

We passed the Hermitage. It was brilliantly lit thanks to a grant from the French government. Then Makarich pointed out the Admiralty steeple. And the Peter-Paul Fortress.

We continued on to see the first of the bridges open.

By one o'clock, the night sky had reached its nadir. It was finally but reluctantly dark except for a subtle, stubborn glow on the horizon.

The bridges began to open at about one thirty, each in turn. We saw six of them, driving dutifully from one to the other.

All the while Makarich talked, his eyes pleading with me to comprehend. He held forth on education, psychology, art, theater, Russian politics and history. I could follow little of it.

"When Assi is with us, let's go over this again," I suggested. "It is important that I understand you."

We walked along a quay on the River Neva and passed a tour boat named, "*Chaika*," The Seagull. We had both acted in the Chekhov play of that name, he as a professional in the major role of Treplev, the aspiring, suicidal playwright. I took a smaller part. I was the tyrannical manager of the estate. Mararich and I had Chekhov and Chaika in common.

In common, too, were our views on education and psychology. "Ah," he said, "our Russian psychologists are so formal. I love the style of you Americans. You leave little distance between yourselves and the children. You are right in there with them."

"It's not 'American psychologists,'" I corrected him. "It's me just as 'Russian psychology' is you. We do things our own way, you and I. You are a different sort of educator. I like to think that I am, too. Certainly, a good educator must break the mold. Don't you think so?"

It was 3:30 a.m. when I finally hit the sack.

- - - - - - - - - - - - - - - - -

The next morning: There are only ten children in Almus today. The rest are on a camping trip. They left last night while Makarich and I were out looking at bridges. We were to join group for a while at the campsite but there had been an outage at St. Petersburg's atomic generating plant. As a result, the *electrichka*, the commuter train that was to take Makarich and me to the camp site, was not in service. Sadly, we were obliged to remain at home.

- - - - - - - - - - - - - - - - -

Anya, the smiling, cognitively handicapped child, is in my kitchen at the moment along with a new girl, Marina, who returned just yesterday from the hospital where she underwent a major operation. I hadn't met her before. I don't have any idea what was wrong with her. She says she doesn't know either. Both girls are ten years old. I hand them unlined paper. They sit quietly and draw while I type.

Their drawings are well done, colorful and attractive.

Every now and again one and then the other gives me a picture on which she has written her name and, "To Bob to remember me by. '*Kak pamlat'*.'" I accept each gift with lavish gratitude.

- - - - - - - - - - - - - - - - -

Let us look at Art. Art is the key to everything. To survive in full humanity, everyone must have something that he or she can do well, something that comes from within, from commitment, from passion rather than duty, something that is the expression of a private vision— yet shared, his or her gift to the world. Each of us has a potential gift to offer, one that comes from the heart unsullied by motives of personal advantage or even the logic of exchange; we are fortunate when we are able to offer our art to others.

Take Zhenya. Zhenya is an artist. His physical grace is singular. He spins effortless cartwheels as we stroll along. "He is like a circus acrobat," Irina Ivanovna noted. If circumstances were to allow it, he would be just that, an acrobat in the circus. He is a remarkable eight-year-old artist.

What if Almus were to offer him an opportunity to develop and display his talent? He might then no longer be known as "the bad boy whose mother doesn't like him."

He would instead be "our most graceful acrobat." And might see himself that way, too.

- - - - - - - - - - - - - - - - -

The children slept all morning. No school. It is *Den' Pobyedy.* Victory Day.

Makarich took me to the Victory Parade on Nevsky Prospekt, St. Petersburg's main avenue. He brought along his friend, Suore, a teacher of English and Suore's wife, Galina, a school psychologist.

The spectacle of aging veterans, heroes of the terrible "Great Patriotic War"—'World War II to the rest of the world—marching with painful, determined steps to the cheers of the crowd, was deeply moving.

"Who *really* won that war?" Suore snorted. "Look how the Germans live today and compare their lives to ours! As for heroes, the 'veterans to whom we are eternally grateful.' Their pensions don't even cover the price of bread."

We adjourned to Makarich's room. He cooked us a delicious veal cutlet dinner. The room is in an apartment shared with I don't know how many other people, a *kommunalka*, an arrangement infamous for contentious living, a pest house where interpersonal conflicts fester and, under the Communists, where petty spying on friends and neighbors was encouraged.

Suore told me that his family had been destroyed by the post-Soviet economy. Both he and Galina are now obliged to take on private students. Even so, their combined income is little more than the equivalent of a hundred dollars a month. They have two children to support.

"Life must have been better under the Communists," I suggested.

"No," he said. "It is better now."

- - - - - - - - - - - - - - - -

After lunch, Makarich drove me back to the priut. We picked up three children there, Zhenya, the younger Andrei, and the pleasant, cognitively impaired, Anya. Together we returned to central city to see the victory fireworks. They began at ten in the evening and would probably have been a first-rate spectacle had it been dark enough by then to see it to full advantage. By ten, it was barely dusk. In a few weeks, there will be no night at all in this great northern city.

- - - - - - - - - - - - - - - -

Andrei, age 12. Andrei is a quiet, cooperative fellow, indeed he is rather passive. But on occasion he turns giddy, never quite out of control but there is a sense of nervous energy behind his placid appearance. He hangs out with Yura, a much younger and far wilder kid. Yura is Andrei's wild side.

I like Almus a lot. I've been here about two weeks. The reason I'm here is I don't want to live at home any more. And the reason I don't is my father hits me. My mother is living someplace with another man. I'm not sure where.

First I lived with my mother and her parents, my grandparents; but then they died and I was moved to my father's place. You see, before my grandfather died, he had asked my father to take me in. So it was just me and my father. It was bad. Real bad.

My father was always drunk when he hit me. His reasons were like, "You went out with your friends and you didn't come home on time!"

So finally I went to the police and asked them to bring me someplace. The police told me about this priut.

What I like about it here is that it's like home. I don't mean the home with my father. I mean my grandparent's house before I lived with my dad. The vospitatilye treat me very well and the kids are all okay.

As to my future, I don't know yet. I won't drink. That much I know. It's no good. You can end up hitting your children who you are supposed to love. If I had a son like me who did what I did, I'd just talk to him. I would never hit him.

When I leave here, my mother will stop drinking and she'll live alone and she'll take me in to live with her. The man she lived with before is in jail now. Now she's got some other guy. I don't know about him. All I know is she promised me she'd stop drinking.

My mother is okay. She doesn't hit. I would really like to go back and live with her.

I want to be a doctor someday. The reason is, when I was sick, doctors took really good care of me. I'm a pretty good student so maybe I can make it.

- - - - - - - - - - - - - - - - -

Zhenya: Assi, my otherwise faultless translator and

assistant, left two cigarette butts in my sitting room ashtray this morning. A few minutes later, Zhenya popped in to say, "*Previet!*" (Hi!). When eventually he left, I noticed that one cigarette butt was missing.

The same thing happened the other day. The older Lyuba swiped a butt that Assi left behind.

I mentioned the butt-stealing events to vospitatilnitsa Tatiana Mikhailovna. She shrugged her shoulders as if to say, "There's nothing to be done about it."

- - - - - - - - - - - - - - - -

Anya: She did not wish to be interviewed. I suspect that she has little confidence in her linguistic skills. (I have little confidence in mine and recognize a soul mate.)

- - - - - - - - - - - - - - - -

Tatiana Michailevna, age 46. Tatiana Mikhailovna is a thoughtful woman who works with children diligently and well. She is earnest and serious to the point of seeming professorial. Yet the children say she can also be quite humorous. They like her and they seem to be at the center of her life.

I've worked here for five years. I began at the old place. Everything about Almus has changed since we were there. Then we were located in a small apartment and the atmosphere was like that of a family. The children and staff were attached to each other. We took our meals together around one big, round table.

We can suggest things to Makarich that might bring back that family feeling. There wouldn't be any special problem if we did, but we have so many questions and suggestions all the time that it is hard to bring everything to his attention and to make it into a key agenda item. Makarich remembers everything. He has a remarkable mind; just like a computer. He can remember every suggestion that we make; but he can't bring them all about. He is a very decent man, very brilliant, and he does his best. What else can we ask?

We work well with our psychologist. Our meetings are really conversations. We tell her what we've noticed about the children and she gives us the results of the testing that she's done with them. Then we compare opinions. It is very good. If we want more information, all we have to do is ask and we get it. She is a very accommodating person.

I used to be an economist. I came here by accident. Once I heard Makarich on the radio. He was talking about a camping club where the children make their own tents and so on. I love camping and it sounded interesting to me. So I called and offered my services as an instructor. They told me there was no job like that but they said I could work here as a vospitatilnitsa. I tried it and loved it.

I quit my job as an economist. It was a good position at the Institute for Research. They were very reluctant to let me go. After I was in Almus for a while, they offered me my old job back but I said that it would be impossible for me to return. My reasons were these: First, I like working at Almus better. Second, in this kind of work, you must throw your total self into it. You have to give it all of your time and energy. There is no time or energy left for anything else.

I continue to enjoy the job but it is very hard. Sometimes

I confess I wish I wasn't doing this. There is no escape. I take it home at night with me.

I'm married and I've adopted a child from here. He is fourteen now. My husband and I don't have our own child. We have many problems with our adopted son. It is not an ideal relationship. He is a quiet boy and he needed a family very much. That is why we adopted him. They were going to send him to a dietskiy dom but I didn't think that an institution would have been right for him.

Communication is essential in Almus. We meet with the new shift each morning. We communicate fully. It is not a formal meeting but we take the time to talk in detail. We have special notebooks for what happens during the entire previous day and night and a second notebook for events that occur only in school. In that notebook we record our meetings with teachers and parents. We also talk with each other a lot on the phone.

Each of us on each shift is assigned particular children to work with. We must give our colleagues on the next shift detailed information on exactly what has been going on with them.

Our main supervisor is Klavdia Aleksandrovna. She is the person we go to for questions or help. We do not go to Makarich so much because we don't want to undercut her.

The basic problem here is that children remain with us for such a brief time. If we could keep them until they become adults, we would be able to raise good citizens.

I think we should organize more clubs, camping clubs,

for example. We do have some good ones already including an art club.

Another key problem is that there is not enough equipment. Last winter we went around to schools to borrow skis and a ping pong table. We know how important it is for children to have the opportunity to participate in sports.

- - - - - - - - - - - - - - - - -

Morning: Klavdia Aleksandrovna arrives. She is the assistant director but I recently learned that her actual title is, "Director of the Second Floor." Children rush to greet her. She folds them in her arms. She is respected by everyone. I, too, see her as excellent in all ways. But I don't quite understand: does her position place her between the director and the children or do she and Makarich constitute a team, a single administrative entity? If it's the latter, fine. If the former, I can imagine occasional conflict. Is there conflict or are they reading from the same page?

- - - - - - - - - - - - - - - - -

I wrote for about an hour and then wandered the halls to see what was going on. It is 10:30 a.m. The half-dozen kids not in school are glued to the television set watching an American hospital drama. People are slugging each other on the screen. The cops arrive and there is a bloody shoot-out.

- - - - - - - - - - - - - - - - -

Tolik marches up and down the corridor back-and-forth-back-and-forth in his bathrobe and slippers. He strides from his room to the playroom where the television is blaring then back to his room again. He repeats the sequence again. And again. And again.

- - - - - - - - - - - - - - - - -

Evening: Eleven o'clock. The television set has been turned off. At last. Natalia Borisovna has six children playing "Simon Says" in the corridor. Yura calls the commands.

Yura has become remarkably civilized. After dinner, the kids had gathered in my room to play on the computer. It was Yura's turn. He did what he always does—shoot down the bad guys. When I told him that his time was up, he relinquished the computer to the next kid with neither fuss nor complaint. What was even more surprising is that I had some *pechen'ya*—cookies—in the room and told the kids that they could each take a few. Yura took no more than a half-dozen and sharply reprimanded Dima for grabbing too many.

By contrast, Tolik behaved badly. He didn't wait his turn on the computer but pulled it unceremoniously away from a little kid whose turn it was.

I let that go without comment but shouldn't have. All the children in the room—seven or eight at the time—were little ones, seven- to ten-year-olds. Not only was Tolik much bigger but he projects an overbearing, angry quality that makes people fearful and keeps them at a distance.

He played on the computer for a very long time. Finally, one of the little Dimas said, "Hey! It's *my* turn now." Tolik ignored him. Dima said it again. No response. I finally intervened. I said, "Tolik, your turn is over. Dima has been waiting. Time to end it."

"Wait, wait," Tolik said. "Wait."

Other kids got into the argument. "Tolik! Let Dima have his turn!" one of them said. "He's a little kid and has to go to bed."

Ten-year-old Yulia was particularly incensed. "We're *all* little kids here. You shouldn't push us around like that."

Tolik made an incoherent reply and exited the room.

- - - - - - - - - - - - - - - - -

Why did the girls pick on the younger Sveta today again on our after-dinner walk? Why did she retreat with neither complaint nor counterattack?

Why was Dima crying?

There are things in this world I shall never understand.

- - - - - - - - - - - - - - - - -

I entered the dining room holding Marina's hand. Marina, age 9, is the sad-eyed recent arrival from hospital. She underwent, and has only recently recovered from, a major operation for a congenital heart defect. The procedure was arranged for by Vrachi Mira and performed by an American surgeon.

Because of this problem, Marina had spent most of her life in bed. She has few social skills and is a highly dependent child, frightened, clingy, odd. The other children are tolerant but for the most part ignore her.

I don't know why I had the operation exactly. I don't know much about it but I know it was on my heart. I'm okay now. I was in the hospital for only a month. Before the operation I used to have bad headaches. I stayed in bed for a long time, for years. I read a lot, mostly grown-up books.

I've been here at Almus for three months. I don't like it that much because I don't get to see my mother. She used to come every day. Now I don't see her that much. She will take me next weekend. My father is in a very secret place with four walls. I think somebody turned him in.

My mother doesn't work. She rents out a room in her apartment. She lives in one room and rents out the rest of it.

My sister is fourteen and lives with my grandmother. My mother doesn't earn much money so she can't afford to feed us and take care of us.

Here's what I like about Almus: I like you, Bob!

When I have free time, I like to draw, read and watch TV. When I grow up, I want to get a job.

Marina and I sat together at a little, four-sided dining room table. She was on my right. The younger Lyuba rushed over and grabbed the seat to my left and announced that the remaining seat, the one between her and Marina, was reserved for Yulya, her best friend. She then went to the serving window to collect her kasha and tea.

While she was doing that, Zhenya, the little wise-guy, plopped himself down in Lyuba's seat. When she returned, she was naturally furious and drove him off with punches and imprecations. But Zhenya didn't go very far. He simply stood behind the seat on his left, the one where Marina had been and informed her in a forceful voice that it now was his. Classic imperialism.

Rather than protest, Marina retreated passively to another table. But young Sveta was already there. Sveta's social skills are also relatively undeveloped but she managed to hold her ground.

That was not the end of it. Nadinka, the omni-competent seven-year-old, decided to join us at the first table. Yulya then, through force of personality combined with an assortment of harsh words, drove Zhenya away from the seat he pilfered from Marina. He retreated meekly just as had Marina, his own victim. Yulya took his place to my right, leaving her own seat to Nadinka. Marina and Zhenya eventually found places at other tables as children finished their meals and danced out of the dining room chirping, *"Spacibo"* to the cooks.

(Apologies, dear reader. The above anecdote is impossible to follow. But that is reality.)

- - - - - - - - - - - - - - - -

"Dobroe utro," good morning. Klavdia Aleksandrovna materialized, framed by the doorway of the staff kitchen, her arms full of good things to eat, home-canned cherries and figs, parsley and sprigs of celery. Soon other vospitatilye arrived. They busied themselves preparing food. In no more than a moment the table was loaded with cakes, tea, jam, coffee and sandwiches.

It was time for the daily morning staff meeting, the

changing of the guard. Yesterday's crew was to bring today's up to speed. Klavdia Aleksandrovna was fully, energetically but convivially in charge. She is a businesslike person but one who laughs easily. There were five vospitatilye present, all women. Over snacks, taking tea, chatting, and laughing together, serious professional matters were discussed.

I could not quite follow the conversation but was aware that it covered the behavior of specific children and incidents that had occurred during the previous twenty-four hours were reviewed.

I suspect that much good was accomplished.

- - - - - - - - - - - - - - - -

I had a meeting with the psychologists. It went off well enough. I would give it a B+. About thirty people attended. The crowd was divided between psychologists and vospitatilye. Makarich chaired. Assi translated.

I offered my opinion that there should be a focus on *program.* That is the key, ultimately far more helpful to the children than is concern with the psyche. At the same time, one must remember that the individual is our ultimate concern albeit in a social context.

I further expressed the view that psychologists would do well to consider the vospitatilye rather than the children their primary clients. Psychologists are best thought of as support staff whose job it is to maximize the effectiveness of those in the trenches. They should focus on listening to and observing the children in their daily activities. The results of this study should render consultation with the vospitatilye both relevant and useful. This is better use of a psychologist's time than to be relegated, cloistered, in a dingy office administering tests or seeking a cure for unhappiness whether through conversation or medicine.

If they were listening, I doubt that anyone left the meeting under the impression that I was arguing against vospitatilye talking freely with children about whatever may be on their minds. To the contrary, I advocated for a pervasive, open, entirely trusting climate throughout the entire institution in which frank conversation and problem solving may occur everywhere, any time, among staff, among children, and between staff and children, not limited to a single venue—not even the psychologist's consulting room.

The child may choose whomever he or she wishes to talk with or to refrain from talking with anybody. Everyone employed by the institution ought to be open to all the children and prepared to respond to any and all with warmth, wit and the utmost seriousness.

The central job of the psychologist, I concluded is, like that of the theater director, to create a scene where something of significance may occur.

- - - - - - - - - - - - - - - - -

Alla Pavlovna seemed to appreciate what I said as did Makarich. Jeff, too. There was at least one psychologist who also seemed to agree with me. My words were probably lost on others, however. In the discussion that followed, someone asked me to discuss scoring issues on the Wechesler Intelligence Scale for Children.

- - - - - - - - - - - - - - - -

After dinner. Little Lyuba and Yulya asked if I would take them for a walk. I of course agreed but added that they would need first to check with Irina Ivanovna, the vospitatilnitsa on duty.

Zhenya and Marina asked if they could join us. Then five or six more kids asked, too.

Irina Ivanovna did not hesitate to agree to the walk in principle but thought that I should limit myself to no more than five children. She proceeded to eliminate those she thought might be too difficult for me to handle as well as those who had uborka to attend to before bedtime. This meant that neither Zhenya nor Marina could go, Zhenya for the former reason and Marina for the latter. Both sobbed pitifully. Because of uborka Svetka wasn't allowed to go either but she took the news stoically.

I left with Lyuba, Yulya, Mariana, Nadya, and Anya in tow.

We wandered down the path to a playground within the housing complex. The children were soon playing a fast game of tag. Cognitively disabled Anya was "it" from the start. She never managed to tag anyone. They all danced away from her whenever she got close, taunting, poking and kicking her from every direction. I noted that even Nadinka, Anya's best friend and protector, joined the cruel sport. Although her tormentors only teased and never bullied or hit her, it must have been an humiliating experience. Anya wore a frozen smile throughout as she swatted in the general direction of anyone within ten feet, her arms swinging like paddle wheels. She ran here and there, sweating, panting but never tagging anyone.

I finally put a stop to it.

Next time we should begin our walk with a review of what's fair and take time to establish rules for the game, compassionate ones. Also: either we take *bad* kids along, or we take no walk at all. Bad kids could be no worse than these good ones. Those who have uborka commitments must, naturally, remain home.

- - - - - - - - - - - - - - - - -

The Last of the Interviews:

Dima, age 7. Dima is a quiet boy; cooperative and helpful. He gets along well with the other younger boys. Often his face projects sadness and it is always pale perhaps because of ill health, depression or an inadequate diet. He is passive, dependent, and marginal. He has a few friends but none with whom he seems to spend much time.

I've been here for about four months. I sort of like it but only a little. What's good about this place is taking walks with you, Bob. What's bad is that I've been here too long. I miss my home.

I'm here because my father doesn't make enough money to take care of me. But I think he is making more money now. I'll do second grade at home. My father will take me home right after the tests here.

My mama is always working. I don't remember what she does. She works in the city somewhere.

I have a cousin. He lives with his own parents.

*I have two friends here, Zhenya and Sasha. The other
kids in Almus are okay. The vospitatilye…. They're okay,
too.*

I like to play Sega games when I am home.

- - - - - - - - - - - - - - - - -

We have interviewed almost everyone now—although
two children did not want me to talk with them about
anything personal. A vospitatilnitsa thinks they have a
history of being sexually abused. One other kid we did
not interview is seven-year-old Sasha. By the time we
were ready for him this evening he was well on his way
to bed. We never got to interview Anya, the cognitively
disabled girl. I did ask her once if she was up for it but
she declined. We also missed the new vospitatilnitsa,
Alexandra Viktorovna, a.k.a. Sasha.

Unbelievably, we haven't yet had a proper interview with
Makarich, one aided by a translator. He is the dominant
presence in this place … and yet …. He is hard to
catch up with.

Or is he elusive?

- - - - - - - - - - - - - - - - -

Pasha and Alyona refused to participate in uborka.
"We are too tired," they complained. The vospitatilye
became insistent at which point the girls got nasty
and screamed at them. It was a scene that I had not
witnessed here until now. Alyona stomped up and down
the corridor. Natalia Nikolaevna followed right behind
her, arguing, demanding, pleading.

Three little kids meanwhile mopped the floors without

incident. Their age-mates were already asleep. It was almost ten PM.

"Why do they need to do their chores at night" Assi wondered, "when everyone is tired?"

"I have no idea," I said.

- - - - - - - - - - - - - - - - -

The children and I wandered around the neighborhood together for the last time this evening. We had a healthy mix of good kids plus a few notoriously bad ones. Prominent members included Yura, the younger Andrei, Marina, the younger Lyuba, and the tranquil Dima.

The occasion for the walk was for us to have one last adventure before I leave for America tomorrow. Difficult-to-handle kids were welcome—the vospitatilye trust me more today than yesterday—but those who had behaved badly *recently* and those burdened with uborka were not permitted to come. Yura got in under the wire. Olga, Tanya Igor'ievna's ten year daughter, came with us. She was a constructive presence; she initiated all sorts of hopping, dancing and singing games. Spirits were high and behavior was exemplary.

Afterwards, children made one last visit to my sitting room where they played on the computer or drew pictures. Yura, the street kid, drew a heart with an arrow through it. I asked a couple of the vospitatilye to guess the artist. They both thought it was done by a sweet little girl.

Vospitatilnitsa Irina Ivanovna interrupted the art session to remind Tolik that he had uborka to do. He announced that he wouldn't. *"Plokho!"* Bad! Alyona and Pasha accused him in chorus.

They twirled their middle fingers against the side of their heads and pointed at him.

"Crazy!" they said.

- - - - - - - - - - - - - - - -

"Tolik paced the floor all night long," Irina Ivanovna said when we had breakfast tea together in the staff kitchen the next morning. He kept the staff awake, walking, walking, walking from one end of the corridor to the other, frantically, nervously, lost in thought, not speaking out loud but mumbling to himself.

- - - - - - - - - - - - - - - -

Soon I must take my leave.

I bought a couple of cakes at the Lomonosovskaya Metro station outdoor market. Just before bedtime we threw a party for all the children. I gave each of them a handful of little plastic toys that had been contributed by Vermonters.

There was a hearty chorus of *"spasibo, Bob!"* (thank you, Bob) followed by countless Russian bear hugs.

- - - - - - - - - - - - - - - -

Down the hall, Mariana, never a crybaby, was bawling. "What happened?" Some of the rough, younger boys had attacked her, she said. I am not sure who they were. Yura, Andrei and the angry Dima, I would guess. The vospitatilnitsa on duty comforted Mariana but I saw no evidence that she was about to seek out the offending boys for a lecture, much less chastisement.

- - - - - - - - - - - - - - - - -

Two new children arrived today while I was downtown, ten-year-old Masha and eight-year-old Vanya. They had been in the isolation ward downstairs for several days. Masha is already friends with most of the girls because she is from the neighborhood. She loves being in Almus, she said. But Vanya cries for his mother. He stuck very close to me. Like some others around here, he wears a sad look on face. "He has problems," Natalia Borisovna said.

- - - - - - - - - - - - - - - - -

The children gathered in my sitting room for the very last time. They drew pictures and gave them to me as presents, "*kak pamiat'*," to remember us by.

There was much begging. "*Why* do you have to leave?"

"*Will* you ever come back?"

"*Will* you write to me?"

"*Will* you take my picture *one* more time?"

"Will you give me a *present*?"

Yura gave me a tiny plastic car.

Mariana gave me a book about Jesus (left at the priut by some missionary).

They all gave me the pictures that they had drawn in my sitting room.

- - - - - - - - - - - - - - - -

There were more good-byes, hugs and promises at breakfast. After the kids who were enrolled in school went on their way, I took whatever others I could find, six in all, for one last, absolutely final, walk. On the way, Losha requested ice cream. "Certainly, my friend," I said. We bought a couple of dozen cones and pops and headed right back to Almus to share them with the other kids.

- - - - - - - - - - - - - - - -

"Pasha," I asked, "where will you go after you leave Almus?"

"Home," she said.

"To your *father?*" I exclaimed, incredulous.

"Yes."

"But you said that he drinks and beats you."

"He used to but maybe he won't any more."

"But, Pasha dear, what if he does it again? What would you *do*?"

"I will come back here," she said. "I *love* it here!"

- - - - - - - - - - - - - - - -

Still more hugs; still more good-byes. I kissed each of the vospitatilye. "You are welcome back any time," Klavdia Aleksandrovna said.

"Maybe next year," I said. "Or maybe you will come to America someday."

"How would I *ever* get to America?" sixteen-year-old Sveta said, wiping her eyes. She hurried out the door for secretarial school.

Marina took my hand, held it tight and kissed it.

Nadinka sat on my lap. She stroked the flabby skin under my jaw. "You are old, Grandpa Bob!" she giggled.

- - - - - - - - - - - - - - - - -

Yura came into my room as I packed. "Give me a *present!*" he ordered.

"I've given out all the presents," I said. "And you got plenty of them."

We wrestled. He punched in the direction of my genitals.

- - - - - - - - - - - - - - - - -

I barged into Losha's room. "Hey, Loshka!" I said. "You forgot to return my slang dictionary! I'm leaving for America in a few minutes."

"Oh, yeah," he said, apparently embarrassed. "Here it is. Sorry."

I was so pleased that he returned it with no game-playing that I handed it back to him.

"A gift," I said. "To remember me by."

"Thank you," he said.

- - - - - - - - - - - - - - - - -

Makarich popped in to bid me farewell. I wanted to say something extravagant but lacked the skill. I wanted to tell him that he has indeed created a family here at Almus. But all I could manage was, "Good luck, my friend, with everything." We shook hands.

Vasy, the DOW chauffeur, showed up with Jeff. They drove me to St. Petersburg's Pulkovo Airport.

2000

When my cab drew up, Makarich—Mikhail Makarievich—was in the driveway, bent under the hood of the priut's green Volga jeep. He rose and we embraced, Russian-masculine style. "Welcome, Bob," he said.

"I am very pleased to be here," I said.

I entered the building with a hearty "*previet,*" hi, to the tall guy with the white mustache, the fellow who lets people in and out of the building, more concierge than guard. Tatiania Viktorovna and Natalia Nikolaevna, vospitatilye I've known since the start of this project, were on duty. We hugged and kissed on the cheeks, three times, *po-ruski,* as is done in Russia.

Alicia and her sister, Anya, now thirteen and fourteen respectively, are back looking almost like grownups. I knew them from my visit two years ago. They had tried living with their mother but it didn't work because, they explained, "she was always drunk." One day Anya just picked up the phone and called Almus to say that they wanted to come back, permission was granted and back they came.

Vanya is here, a fellow who had just arrived as I departed last year. He was very homesick at the time and cried a lot. Now he looks like one of the group. I asked him how he likes Almus.

"It's nice," he said with moderate conviction.

Someone else from last year, Sveta, now seventeen years old, struck me then and impresses me now as unusually mature, both physically and personally. She works elsewhere during the day and sleeps here at night. She is waiting for her deceased grandmother's room in a kommunalka to be available to her. It is to be renovated after which she will take possession and move in.

- - - - - - - - - - - - - - - -

An update from vospitatilnitsa Natalia Borisovna:

Much has changed since last year. We are reorganizing. The older children are now living in a cluster of rooms down the corridor, separated from the younger residents by a door that is often locked. Each group has its own program. There are now three vospitatilye who work exclusively with the older kids. The new arrangement is good for everyone, the younger ones, the older ones, and the vospitatilye.

The older kids cook their own meals every evening. We help them. Then we discuss their plans for the next day with them. They now have a wider choice activities and hobbies. Some like drawing, some like to work with clay. They all love to travel and last year we went on a wonderful winter camping trip to Murmansk.

There is a good and harmonious atmosphere between

*the vospitatilye and the teenagers. We don't have
television so we talk with each other and just spend a
lot of time together. All of us consider those to be the
most important parts of our daily lives. If we ask for the
kids to help with just about anything, they do so willingly.
They work a lot with the younger children and become
like big brothers and sisters to them.*

*My own role has changed. I now work with the Vrachi
Mira social worker on adoptions and foster care. We
have successfully placed six of the little children in
foster families.*

Things are much better now.

- - - - - - - - - - - - - - - - -

When her shift ended, I walked Natalia Nikolaevna to
the Metro. "In some ways life is getting better in Russia,"
she said in response to my question. "In some ways
worse. Children don't read any more."

Earlier today, Natalia Nikolaevna had taken the children
to hear Mozart's Requiem at the St. Petersburg
Philharmonic Hall.

"It is important to expose them to culture," she said.

- - - - - - - - - - - - - - - - -

The two vospitatilye, Tatiana Viktorovna and a new
woman, Ina—her otchestvo did not stick in my mind—
who smiles easily, invited me to tea. Ina had been co-
leader on the trip to hear Mozart's *Requiem*.

"The children were completely bored," she reported.
"They don't understand classical music."

- - - - - - - - - - - - - - - - -

Vospitatilnitsa Tatiana Viktorovna asked seven-year-old Katya to accompany me to the dining room. It was to be a way of welcoming me and an honor for her. Katya came to my room to get me. She gently took my hand and we galloped together, first down the corridor and then the steps.

Cutlets and cabbage on tonight's menu. Not bad, a bit bland perhaps but not bad at all. Healthy.

For some reason, little Oleg was in tears. Tatiana Viktorovna sat close to him, rubbed his shoulders and whispered something soothing to him.

"What was the matter?" I asked later. "He's new," she said, "and he misses his mother. He won't eat. He says he doesn't like cabbage."

- - - - - - - - - - - - - - - - -

Tatiana Viktorovna was in charge again at bedtime for the younger children. They swept and mopped the floor—normal daily uborka. But chubby Pashka, a tear inching toward his chin, stood alone in the hallway, facing the wall.

"He doesn't want to do *anything*," Tatiana Viktorovna explained. "He won't eat, participate in uborka, or go to bed." She shrugged as if to say, "What is to be done with such a fellow?"

- - - - - - - - - - - - - - - - -

As they finished their uborka, children drifted into my

sitting room to play games on my new laptop. "Are they bothering you?" Tatiana Viktorovna asked, sticking her head in at the door. "You must have your own work to do."

"This *is* my work," I said.

- - - - - - - - - - - - - - - - -

Anya and Alicia followed me around all day, dogging my footsteps. They remembered many details from our adventures two years ago including a computer game they especially liked. "I don't have those games any more," I said. "But I have some great new ones."

"Can we play them?"

"Of course!"

- - - - - - - - - - - - - - - - -

Oleg and his roommate, Anton, both nine, drew pictures and donated them to me just before they went off to bed. I hung them on my wall. Oleg's was of a peaceful scene. A bright sun was in the sky. A truck made its way along a green, country road. On its roof was a flag that had on it the inscription, "USA." An airplane flew by.

Anton's was of a tank bristling with eleven guns and almost as many rockets.

- - - - - - - - - - - - - - - - -

Before breakfast, the vospitatilye invited me to join them in their kitchen for pre-breakfast tea, cakes, salami sandwiches, and gossip. I ate well but, as is usually the case, could not quite follow the conversation.

Afterwards, Oleg wandered into my room to play some more computer games. Then it was breakfast time in the dining room. A cream of wheat *kasha* (cereal) was served along with bread, both dark and white, cheese, and tea.

Alicia asked me to sit at her table. She dished kasha into my bowl. Other children gathered around, some asked questions about America, some made comments, while others simply stood there, looking me over, checking me out.

"Do you know the Spice Girls?" someone asked.

"What do you think of Britney Spears?" a little girl inquired shyly.

Alicia was in her administrative mode. She handled me with the skill of an impresario. She and her sister, Anya, carry themselves now with a confidence and authority that I do not recall from previous visits.

Alicia said, "Tatiana Igor'ievna, Natalia Borisovna, and Irina Ivanovna will be the vospitatilye on duty today. Isn't that great?"

After breakfast, Oleg said that he wanted to play games on my computer yet again. It is getting to be a bit much. "I have work to do," I said with exaggerated weariness.

"*PazhAHlusta!*" Pleeease.

"But...well... okay. Maybe just a few minutes." He raced into my room. Other children followed. They gathered around the computer. Everybody, children and vospitatilye, is in an energetic mood today.

It was time for school—for those enrolled locally. Tatiana Viktorovna popped her head in my door and announced, "School! Let's go!" The children departed at once with a hearty "good-bye" and "may we play on your computer again this evening?"

- - - - - - - - - - - - - - - - -

Klavdia Aleksandrovna, the Director of the Second Floor, is chief vospitatilnitsa. She invited me to the morning tea meeting with members of today's vospitatilye shift.

As is customary in this priut if not everywhere in Russia, the business meeting was embellished with fish sandwiches, tea, cookies, cake and bagels. There were three vospitatilye present, Irina Ivanovna, Natalia Borisovna, Tatiana Igor'ievna. It was hosted, of course, by Klavdia Aleksandrovna herself who presided over the discussion with grace and good humor.

The details were over my head but it was clear that they went over specific children and their problems, family and personal. It did not seem that they were concerned with yesterday's behavioral issues so much as what each of them need to think about when they work with the families.

The implicit goal of the meeting, I suspect, was to enhance vospitatilye morale and the sense of working together. It felt like a gathering of friends more than a formal meeting.

- - - - - - - - - - - - - - - - -

Some of the children who do not go to school are back in their rooms now. I am not sure what they are doing but I shall go and take a peek.

Not much is going on. I will check downstairs.

- - - - - - - - - - - - - - - - -

The children are at work with a young tutor whom I have not yet met. I see her walking with her arms around two little girls. The three are chirping gaily about something—I know not what. She is fully engaged with the children, a heartening sight. Over and over again I find that, apart from the retreats to their kitchen for tea, the vospitatilye work warmly and sensitively with the children.

The kids are in a particularly up-beat mood today, and seem to require little supervision. For the most part they are grateful for almost everything that is done for or with them. "Thank you for the walk, *Dya-dya Bob* (Uncle Bob). When will you take us on another one?"

Mother Russia—at least Priut Almus—seems to be serving these, her children, quite well.

- - - - - - - - - - - - - - - -

After dinner, Tatiana Igor'ievna and I took eight children for a long walk. It began with some tears because, as is usually the case, a few had unfinished uborka to do and were thus obliged to remain behind.

We strolled through the maze of the high-rise, architecturally insignificant, apartment buildings, along muddy paths and grassy spaces and then along the bank of the fabled Neva. We ran and held hands and took photographs. A kindly couple borrowed my camera and took one of all of us with our arms around each other, mostly smiling but a few kids made goofy faces. We didn't return home until 9:30 and the children didn't get to sleep until well after ten, not good policy on a school night.

I like the way Tatiana Igor'ievna handles children. She chases them, laughs when they say something funny and generally plays it like a big sister. Yet they respect her and she keeps them in good order. She also plays young mother, attentive, a bit on the bossy side, and always high-spirited.

- - - - - - - - - - - - - - - -

My translator for the day was Anton, a student of twenty-three who is aiming to become a professional linguist. He is learning Finnish at the same time as English.

Anton helped me get through a formal meeting, a "*concillium*," which seems to mean a time to consider organizational issues pertaining to children. Cases were not discussed. The agenda included the use of space, and arrangements that must be made when a child leaves the institution; practical matters.

In attendance were about a dozen social workers from a number of organizations. The chairperson was a Mr. Kahn, who, although not overtly controlling, somehow managed to provide little opportunity for discussion. The group energy was low.

Afterwards Anton and I took Mr. Kahn aside and talked with him. He told us about the "family care groups" that are now in operation. This is a tentative form of foster care that allows for adoption if things work out, probably devastating to the child if they don't. For the most part, however, children return eventually to their natural families. Ninety percent of them do, he said. This may be viewed as satisfactory but Mr. Kahn said that usually little is done meanwhile to improve the situation at home. Often the child simply goes back to a bad scene and problems resume.

- - - - - - - - - - - - - - - - -

Vospitatel Sasha—Alexander Viktorovich—organized a gardening crew. My old friend, dark-haired Anya and three of the older children including Yula, a younger girl, plus two preadolescent boys, raked and hauled fallen leaves. They also turned the soil with spades and pitch forks. Tomorrow they will plant trees.

- - - - - - - - - - - - - - - - -

After dinner seven girls and I took a walk. We arrived at a distant playground I had not known before. They scrambled aboard a wildly dangerous, hand-powered Ferris wheel—like contraption. Five teen aged girls from the neighborhood stood by, observing us. They cracked jokes and asked me all sorts of questions about America and who I was and why I was in St. Petersburg. For some reason they did not seem interested in making contact with the Almus girls, possibly because most of the latter were younger.

The locals talked and gigged together in their tight little group. Their tone did not seem hostile so much as self-protective. I remained close to the Almus girls out of loyalty. I did take one picture of the locals but, for balance, a lot more of the Almus gang.

Although older, the neighborhood girls seemed more bedraggled than did ours. One had rotten teeth. All of them wore old clothes. The Almus kids by contrast looked almost privileged.

On our way home to the priut, there was much hand-holding, skipping and racing. I offered shoulder rides as I frequently do if the children are not too big. It was a joyful trip. Vieka met her aunt along the way who was out walking her dog. We stopped to chat with her.

- - - - - - - - - - - - - - - - -

A Vrachi Mira social worker took me on a visit this evening to an adoptive family. Anya, the cognitively disabled girl I met last year, is their newest adoptee along with her older brother whom I do not know. A younger brother may be taken in soon as well. Neither boy is handicapped. The family has adopted yet another child and have a biological son of thirteen, the same age as Anya's older brother. They also have a twenty-five-year-old man living there with his wife. They adopted him as a child. In addition to all those people, they have dogs, cats, puppies, kittens, a parrot, and a tank full of fish. A menagerie.

Father, a reticent fellow, is a factory worker. He earns very little money.

Mother said she takes in all those people and animals to provide an island of humanity in a terrible world. It is her way of doing her part, a quasi-religious calling. Financial support beyond father's salary consists of a tiny government stipend, the equivalent of thirty dollars a month. They manage by making many sacrifices.

Anya said she loves living there.

- - - - - - - - - - - - - - - -

The other Anya and her sister, Alicia, left today for a dietskiy dom. They expected that the move would not occur until next week. They don't know much about the place but heard that it is a good one. They are looking forward to having a permanent home.

Zhenya, a new kid for me, will be gone tomorrow. It happens to be her tenth birthday. I asked Klavdia Aleksandrovna if I might buy ice cream today for everyone to celebrate her birthday in style.

'No," she said. "We don't celebrate birthdays here. If we did, we would need to do it for everyone and we don't have the resources."

Why would that be? Whatever the practical problems, rituals are important for children. Without them to mark significant events, time fades and the self has trouble emerging.

- - - - - - - - - - - - - - - -

It is bothering me. Look: Today is Zhenya's birthday, the very day that she is to move to a dietskiy dom. But there is to be *no ceremony* for either event. Yesterday when Anya and her sister, Alicia, left for their dietskiy dom there was no fuss for them either. Very unfortunate. But Klavdia Aleksandrovna assured me that when children leave, she does give them each an album of all the photographs the priut has of them—including the ones I have taken.

This bothers me too: Last night at her adoptive home, the mildly handicapped Anya had none of the photos that I gave her last year. Where *are* they?

- - - - - - - - - - - - - - - - -

Later: Apologies. I misunderstood. There was indeed a ritual of departure. After breakfast, Klavdia Aleksandrovna ushered the children into the playroom. She had each of them bid farewell to the departing Zhenya. Klavdia Aleksandrova then presented her with gifts, a little toy for her plus a photo album with pictures of her and her Almus friends in it. "To remember us by," she said.

Confession: The night before, I, believing that Zhenya would go uncelebrated, gave her a tiny bottle of Vermont maple syrup, a cassette of rock and roll songs for children, a small package of crayons and a few sheets of paper. She thanked me but remained tense and preoccupied.

"Are you sad, Zhenka?" I asked. "No," she said but her face suggested otherwise. She listened to the cassette on my tape recorder as tears gathered in her eyes. She said that she did not know anything about this new place they were about to bring her to. She referred to it as "another priut," not a "dietskiy dom."

As we talked, her friends joined us, first Lehrer, then the other Zhenya, then Natasha.

Lehrer stroked Zhenya's hair and gave her a photograph

of herself "to remember me by." Natasha gave her a little toy car. I took another photograph.

Later I learned that Zhenya is being sent to the reputedly first-rate Children's Village run by a respected organization, "SOS." I had visited one of its dietskiy doma near Moscow and thought it was a fine place.

I shared my opinions with Zhenya and told her whatever I knew … given my linguistic limitations.

- - - - - - - - - - - - - - - -

More children will be leaving Almus soon. Besides the departure of Anya, Alicia, and Zhenya, Yan said that he will be going home in a few days. There may be others. Empty places will result. Without a constant population, it is hard to get much off the ground.

"We don't worry about having enough residents," Tatiana Viktorovna assured me. "As long as life is hard for parents, Almus will be overflowing with children."

It is a pity that they can't remain for as long as they wish to or may need to.

- - - - - - - - - - - - - - - -

Pasha fought with Anton this morning and sulked off afterward. He refused to go to school. Anton for his part thrives on attention, good or bad, from children or adults. It brings him out of the state of oblivion where he may usually be found.

Anton gave me a drawing when I first arrived on this visit.

I took a group of seven children for a walk after dinner. Pasha and Dima, two particularly difficult fellows, came along. Pasha was okay but Dima was extremely annoying. He repeatedly stuck his face right in front of the camera lens and tickled everybody in the most obnoxious way. He does not relate well to other children. Or to me.

Two of the girls, little ones, held my hands going and returning. Natasha kissed me goodnight on both cheeks—hard—when we got back. Anya, her roommate, hid under the covers. I pulled the blanket down a bit and kissed her on the forehead. She giggled.

The priut was low on bread. So, Tatiana Viktorovna and I accompanied six children, Vieka, Oksana, Lehrer, Dima, Vanya and Yan, on a hike to a distant bakery. The kids alternately ran and walked arm in arm with Tatiana Viktorovna and me and held our hands. The two older girls, Vieka and Oksana, kept close to Tatiana Viktorovna all the while gabbing away in animated voices. Lehrer held onto my right hand. Sometimes one or another of the boys grabbed my left. It was a good start.

On our return home, things became difficult. Oksana, who had banged up her foot the other day and still had a slight limp, began to pout and complain about how tired she was. She insisted that we all take the bus the rest of the way. Vieka, noisily joined in her demand. Meanwhile, Vanya and Dima meowed and screeched like cats for no apparent reason. Dima, who does not relate well to anybody, child or adult, sprinted a hundred yards ahead of us.

Tatiana Viktorovna handled the children gently but firmly and managed to herd everyone as far as a playground that contained exciting, indeed dangerous, equipment on which the children expended their surplus energy.

We resumed our trek. I gave Lehrer a ride on my shoulders followed by turns to each of the others except Oksana who announced haughtily that she wasn't interested. She was too big for me anyway.

Oksana is a moody person. She operates in two modes, one friendly, the other withdrawn. The two alternate without warning. She walked behind the group for a while, her head down. "What is the matter, Oksana?" I asked. "Nothing," she grumbled. An instant later she was dancing alongside us, shouting merrily about what? I haven't a clue.

Dima is our biggest challenge. He has an annoying way of invading other people's personal space and does so *ad nauseum*. He sticks his nose millimeters from that of his victim and then laughs provocatively. He irritates everybody.

Tatiana Viktorovna simply instructed him to walk with the group. He did so. For a few minutes.

I don't know if Tatiana Viktorovna noticed Oksana's dysphoric moods or if she would have chosen to do anything about them if she had. Although skilled and warm, vospitatilye tend not to focus on the internal emotional climate of a child but rather on their behavior. That is not always the case, certainly. It is more a tendency, an inclination.

On our hike, we ran into one of the local girls whose picture I took the other day. Although she has a pretty face, framed with dark, flowing hair, almost every one of her teeth is rotten. She was walking along the Neva with her mother, father, brother and sister. I happened to have her photograph with me. I handed it to her.

She thanked me. Her parents were particularly pleased. Her father reached into his pocket and offered me a handful of coins. I waved him off. "A gift from America," I said.

It is the morning of Russian Orthodox Easter. I am about to take two children to a rehearsal of a street circus program that is to take place in a community center in downtown St. Petersburg. The vospitatilye selected Lehrer and Serogia for the trip, both of whom are nine and neither of whom were deemed too difficult for me to handle.

Serogia is a quiet boy who often wears a pained expression. Lehrer smiles easily.

We will leave Almus at 8:30—*pol devyatovo*. It is now only eight. We have time. My sitting room is still full of this morning's visitors, children who are drawing and messing around. The usual scene. Little Natasha sits beside me doing nothing, my left arm enfolding her.

Later: As planned, I took the two children, first by bus and then by Metro to the *Ploshchad' Vostanniya* (Insurrection Square) Station. From there we grabbed a taxi to the basement of a neighborhood club in some distant neighborhood where the circus workshop was to take place.

No one was there.

After almost an hour, Natalia Nikolaevna, a local woman, showed up with her tiny circus dog. Then a ten-year-old girl showed up to practice gymnastics.

Natalia Nikolaevna explained that the program has fallen on hard times financially. There was now only enough money left for two more months of work. She herself has been paid so little—five hundred rubles a month, the equivalent of about fifteen dollars—that she has been looking for a better job. However, children do continue to show up. The reason that only one person came today is that it is Orthodox Easter Sunday. I hadn't realized that. There is little emphasis on religious holidays at Almus.

Natalia Nikolaevna worked for over an hour with Serogia, Lehrer and the neighborhood girl. She had them jumping through hoops, doing somersaults, cartwheels, flips, and back arches. Serogia was very good at everything, a quick learner, graceful, and by far the best of the three.

This was only the fourth visit here for the local girl. She was not a bad gymnast having learned much previous to her attendance here.

Lehrer was shy at first but eventually participated and became more animated. She mastered a cartwheel.

Natalia Nikolaevna demonstrated the skills of her little dog, *Kroshka*—meaning "Little Hat"—to the delight of the children and me. Wearing a comical red bonnet, Kroshka ran, jumped through hoops, sat up and begged. Cute.

- - - - - - - - - - - - - - - -

On the way home, Serogia, Lehrer and I ate lunch at a fast-food *blini* (pancake) restaurant called *"Skaska,"* Fairy Tale. The kids had never been to a restaurant before and had no idea how to order but they quickly caught on and ended by stuffing themselves with blinis. For desert, Serogia ordered ice cream and Lehrer, a package of chewing gum.

- - - - - - - - - - - - - - - -

A new Anya slouched into my room. She is eleven years old. This afternoon most of the other children went to a circus—not the street circus just discussed but a troupe brought to the priut by a group of evangelical missionaries from America whom I did not have the pleasure of meeting. Anya was lined up to join them but for some reason burst suddenly into whimpering tears that lasted for a very long time. She was sent back to the priut to recover.

Tatiana Yegorovna confided that Anya misses her mother and had threatened to run away to her but was told that it would be best for her to stay. Mother is not willing to take her back just now. Anya claims to like Almus well enough but is very homesick.

I asked Anya to tell me about it but could not make sense of what she said because of a combination of my limited Russian and her sobs. Clearly she did not want to talk about it.

At the moment Anya is playing with my tape recorder, alternately singing into it and chatting. She said that all her grandparents are dead. I offered to be her American grandfather. She sang "Uncle Bob is my grandfather" into the tape recorder over and over again.

Anya has a pretty smile and an endearing manner but she is a real baby and needs to be held, emotionally more than physically.

The next day: I asked Anya about yesterday's homesickness. She could barely recall how sad she was. She is happy at the moment. She, like many children, lives in the present.

- - - - - - - - - - - - - - - -

I sometimes wonder if the personalities of vospitatilye blend into a single Vospitatilnitsa in the minds of the children. Although vospitatilye know much about each child, children must fuse in their minds to become a single Child. If that is true, I wonder if it has any significance in the real world or if it serves to reduce the likelihood of significant personal attachment.

So many children, so many comings and goings, yet every child possesses an unique, well-etched personality and a strong sense of who he or she is. Does this observation hold more true here in Russia than among children from similar circumstances at home? Does our culture produce such distinctive characters? In America we seek our reflections in the flickering images of Beautiful People who are also Extremely Rich.

Perhaps it is otherwise in Russia. Perhaps here the individual person, despite rumors to the contrary, is indeed treasured. Were it otherwise so many unique personalities would not be found. Individuality thrives in this land, certainly in this priut, among the young and maybe within other generations as well.

- - - - - - - - - - - - - - - -

I try to be equally nice to all the children but naturally I find myself feeling closer to some than to others. Homesick Anya is one of my current favorites. Natasha—or "Natalia" as she prefers to be called—is another. They are both in my sitting room as I type. They are singing into the tape recorder and making up silly songs.

"Favorites," is a fluid category. Tomorrow I might add or subtract a kid or two. By the end of my visit here, most of the children will have earned the honor. Some may be unpleasant young people or extremely difficult ones with but many among them are also my favorites.

It is fine to *have* favorites—but not to *play* favorites. In the natural flow of things one comes to know some people better and to feel closer to some. It can't be helped. Having favorites is not a problem. But *playing* favorites is invariably a problem. It can be helped.

- - - - - - - - - - - - - - - -

I type slowly, lost in a cloud of thought. I rise, fuss with the furniture, gather things, file things, arrange things, tape children's drawings to the walls and doors. The children draw. I type on the the computer. We hardly talk. It is a workshop here, a studio, an atelier, a living room; the mood is pensive, inward-looking. The presence of others is lightly felt yet reassuringly, unobtrusively present. The cookie jar is on the shelf.

This is how life should be: family, home, Mr. Rogers' Neighborhood.

This is what mental health looks like. Unfortunately, medications are easier to administer.

- - - - - - - - - - - - - - - -

Programs ought to be in place that are attractive enough to draw children to learn skills without compulsion, any skills. The street circus program was a first-rate example. The children learned a great deal in a very short time because it was an interesting program, not because of anticipated rewards or punishments.

- - - - - - - - - - - - - - - -

Yan, a kid with slightly swarthy skin, perhaps because of Caucasian ancestry, asked me to give him a copy of the Vermont-made "Re-Bops Rock and Roll" cassette tape. I brought a bunch with me to hand out.

"Sorry," I said. "I am not giving out presents yet."

"But you gave one to *Anya*," he whined.

"No," I explained. "That was not a gift. She cleaned my room as a gift. So I gave her a gift back."

"Can *I* clean your room?"

"Of course. It would be great if you did."

"If I do, will you give me a cassette?"

"Yes. Of course."

"Can I do it now?"

"I think it would be better if you did it during uborka time after dinner."

"I'll come back."

Yan did not return after dinner. Other children showed up including Natasha and Anya, my regulars. But not Yan. Not only didn't he show up but he left the photograph of himself in my sitting room. That was my earlier gift to him, a picture he really liked.

Yan's problem is that, like many children his age particularly those from chaotic circumstances, he is a person of the moment. He doesn't carry a thought or a desire into the future. He doesn't think ahead. He doesn't remember. He is a prisoner of his impulses.

As I write this, Yan wanders into my kitchen/sitting room again. I point his failings out to him. "Oh, yes," he says. "I forgot. Where is the photograph?"

"Over there," I say pointing to the kitchen shelf where it lies on top of a pile of papers.

"Oh," he said. "I'll be back tonight to clean your room. Can I listen to the tapes now?"

"No computer games, though. I'm working." He remained in the salon, tape recorder blasting.

- - - - - - - - - - - - - - - -

Earlier that afternoon Yan, rather than participating in uborka, followed me everywhere begging me to take photographs of him.

I took one. Then two. Then three. But it wasn't enough.

"Please, Uncle Bob," he said. "Just *one* more picture. *Please!*"

"Okay," I said, always pleased to be asked. But he never returned to clean my room.

- - - - - - - - - - - - - - - - -

Dima is far more difficult than Yan. He has even less self control. Rather than merely begging, he simply takes whatever attracts him. He marches into my room and lays his grimy hands on my camera, my tape recorder, toys, books, computer. Anything. Everything. Yesterday, while Zhenya played a computer game, Dima pushed some button and the game disappeared from the screen, score unrecorded.

Zhenya howled. He was furious. So was I. "Out!" I yelled.

Normally it is hard to get rid of this kid. He resists physically and then sneaks right back in again. But this time he could see that I really meant it and he slouched off.

Dima has positioned himself outside of civilized society. Children and adults alike keep their distance. He sits alone in the dining room.

Although I throw him out of my sitting room, I also try to offer him inclusion when I can. I took several particularly fine pictures of him yesterday and handed him prints today. I could see that he appreciated them. Photographs are a good present for Dima who has only the vaguest sense of who he is—especially of his positive qualities. Good portraits suggest exactly how one is viewed by the photographer and are extremely helpful in this sort of work but only, of course, if the images are complimentary. I try to make them so.

Anya, the girl who cleaned my room, is, like Dima, impulsive, a person of the moment, and marginal to the social scene. She is also forever in need of assurance.

- - - - - - - - - - - - - - - - -

Confession: I hit my first Russian kid today. It was Dima. I didn't hit him hard. It was just a light tap and I probably wouldn't have hit him at all had my language skills been better. But I was mad and wanted to get a message across.

The problem, I think, is that while Dima has been making a real effort to improve or at least to please, his compulsion to provoke is hard for him to overcome.

What happened is this: After breakfast, Dima and three other boys were playing quietly on my computer. I was impressed with how well behaved Dima was. Unfortunately, when it was time for us to take our walk, he lurched and grabbed, first at my camera and then at my computer, laughing maliciously.

I yelled, "*Nyet! Nyet!*" But firm though I was, I had no effect.

So, I snapped and slapped him ... lightly, I swear, but my anger was palpable. I threw him out of the office, bodily.

Dima ran down the hall, laughing, hid in his room, slammed the door, and burst into bitter tears. I asked him to come out and go on the walk with me and the other kids. He moaned that didn't want to. Perhaps if I had tried harder, he might have been convinced. But I was not well motivated.

The other children and I went out as planned and returned an hour ago. Natalia Nikolaevna told me that Dima is now "*normal'no*," okay. I will try to speak with him when I find a moment.

Later it was as if nothing changed. Dima caught sight of me in the hallway and raced immediately to the door of my room, tried to pry it open before I got out my key unlock it, and behaved once again in his customary giddy, provocative manner. Nothing had changed with this guy.

- - - - - - - - - - - - - - - -

The vospitatilye and I took bedtime tea together. They assured me that they, too, find Dima to be very difficult but, they added, his brother, who had been here a few years ago, is far more so.

Dima was unusually quiet today. Could it have been the result of my having thrown him out of my room by the scruff of the neck again this morning? He snuck back in just as I was leaving and tried to hide from me in the bedroom closet.

- - - - - - - - - - - - - - - -

My sixteen-year-old volunteer translator, Masha, dropped in to help me interview Makarich. An interview with Makarich at long last! But I asked if she would be willing first to help me talk with Dima. Masha aspires to be a psychologist so was more than pleased to try.

I found Dima again and invited him into my sitting room.

I apologized for flying off the handle but also pointed out how frustrating it was to have to worry about all my precious equipment whenever he is around.

He listened closely. We agreed that we want to be friends. I told him that I don't hold grudges. He said that that he now understands the problem and promised not to be such a jerk ("*durok*").

I asked him why he is living in the priut. "My parents threw me out of the house," he said.

"Why?"

"They are drunk all the time. So I run away all the time. And they beat me for it when they find me. Finally, they threw me out."

We shook hands and agreed to be friends. I massaged his shoulders. He dusted off my computer. Then he carefully closed its cover.

- - - - - - - - - - - - - - - - -

After finishing with Dima, Masha and I searched for Makarich. His secretary told us that he had just left for a meeting. Looks like we blew it. My understanding of Almus is incomplete without Makarich's input. I have interviewed almost everyone else. Makarich and I never seem to be in the same place at the same time. I *must* catch up with him. He is the Wizard of Oz, the Great White Whale. I *will* catch up with him. Sooner or later.

- - - - - - - - - - - - - - - - -

What kids need is Program. Program, Program, Program, something constructive that will capture their imaginations at the moment and subsequently increase their ability to focus over time, give them a sense of who they are now and who they are becoming, a sense of continuity, a sense of time. They need something that requires planning and leads successfully to a future event whether it be a theater presentation, an excursion, or the creation of an enterprise. They need to have something to look forward to. They need history.

- - - - - - - - - - - - - - - -

The program for the new, older kids' unit is coming along well. A good example, I am told, was last winter's camping trip to Murmansk. Now, I think, more attention needs to be given to equivalent programming for the younger children.

- - - - - - - - - - - - - - - -

Anya's grandmother died. I am referring here neither to the clingy Anya nor to the one who moved to the dietskiy dom the other day with her sister, Alicia. We have still another Anya, a nine-year-old who has many friends. This is a nation of Anyas. I think Russia suffers from a shortage of female names. This particular Anya had lived with her grandmother for a long time before coming here. The grandmother, according to the vospitatilye, was a good woman who, sadly, drank a lot.

A few minutes ago this Anya tried to call her grandmother. She was told bluntly by the person who answered the phone that her grandma was dead.

Anya threw herself into arms of the vospitatilnitsa,

Tatiana Ivanovna, and sobbed for a long time. Tatiana Ivanovna held her, rocked her and talked soothingly to her.

Later I noticed this Anya in Klavdia Alexandrovna's office. Klavdia Aleksandrovna held her hand and looked into her eyes while the two of them were in deep conversation.

- - - - - - - - - - - - - - - - -

I visited a dietskiy dom this afternoon. It was recommended to me by Vrachi Mira as perhaps the best in St. Petersburg.

The dietskiy dom was housed in a looming, gray building and had long, dark corridors inside. A total of over three hundred children lived there, most of them in that facility. It has two other venues as well.

There was much to praise. The orphanage offers many programs, many of them run smoothly. It is serious about educating the children. Graphic arts, though conventional. are strong as are ceramics, sewing and woodworking. There is a computer lab run by a warm, intelligent man. And the school owns twenty-two computers. All the children's files are in a computer database.

Many specialists are employed including two psychologists, several "social pedagogues" and a few "logotherapists."

When I dropped by her office, one of the psychologists was administering a "WISC"—Wechsler Intelligence Scale for Children—to a young boy. All sorts of tests are given here, including a Russian standardization of the

MMPI—the Minnesota Multiphasic Personality Inventory. Many of these are scored by computer. Because it is so advanced, the dietskiy dom is about to become a training center for psychologists.

The beds in the dormitory were faultlessly made. Everything was sparkling clean. Toys and other objects not in use were arranged neatly on shelves.

I peeked into the dining room. I visited living rooms in each of the age-graded units. I visited classrooms and spoke briefly to teachers. Then the director invited me into his office, first having me wait for some fifteen minutes at his long desk while he made telephone calls and shot off a fax or two.

Impressive. Staff members were proud of what they had accomplished.

I spoke with a fifteen-year-old boy who had been here for four years. He likes it, he said. One summer he went on a bicycle trip to England and was taken in by an English family that he still hears from. He speaks English beautifully.

It is a great institution all right. But I would have preferred a homier atmosphere.

For all I know, despite the technology, the specialists, the tidiness, the computerized tests and the databases, the children themselves might perceive the place as homey. But compared to Almus, it is not.

Russians are by nature a warm, generous people who suffer from the belief that they should be otherwise: efficient, modern and ruthless in order to "catch up" to the West. That's an old story, older than Stalin, Peter the Great, even Ivan the Terrible.

In the meantime, some of us in the West have moved on to celebrate the virtues of conviviality and to question mere professionalism.

Advice to Russia: Drop computerized psychodiagnostics and concentrate instead on supporting natural families by making available to all children, especially those in crisis, such community-based supplements to the family as the Priut Almus programs.

Advice to America: Follow the same lead.

- - - - - - - - - - - - - - - -

I closed the door to my room, sat down at the computer to work on my notes when, without so much as a tap at the door, homesick Anya walked in. A moment later, she was followed by Yan. They wanted to play computer games. "Sorry, kids," I said. "I need to do my work. Come back later."

They wouldn't budge. "Let us play quietly," Yan begged. "We won't bother you."

I relented. It turned into a lovely interlude for the fifteen minutes before dinner. Anya played with an Almus doll's house while Yan listened to Re-Bop songs. I typed away on the computer.

- - - - - - - - - - - - - - - -

Emotionally, the girls around here are a fragile lot; but the boys are, with rare exceptions, sadder. As a group, they tend to be infantile, restless and unanchored.

Maybe this is because most teachers and vospitatilye are women who worry about female things: Is this child eating? Is that one dressed for the cold?

Alexander Viktorovich—"Sasha"—and a new vospitatel, Boris Borisovich, deal with children differently. Sasha creates tasks and programs. Boris gets kids moving. Women create a sense of care and order.

- - - - - - - - - - - - - - - - -

Sometimes attempts at control are confusing. Yesterday at lunch three separate vospitatilye sternly instructed the children to behave but each was concerned with a different aspect of behavior. One told the children to eat, another thought that they should talk in more modulated tones, and the third attempted to keep them from jumping out of their seats.

"You have many mothers here," I said to Vieka, the liveliest of the girls whom all three vospitatilye surely must have had in mind in all their instructions.

"Yes," she sighed.

- - - - - - - - - - - - - - - - -

Alla Pavlovna came over this evening with a certain Natasha in tow, a bright young psychologist she hired to help create a foster care program. Alla is thinking of quitting Vrachi Mira and believes that Natasha would make a good replacement although she is only twenty-five years old.

Natasha is well educated and has a solid grasp of issues related to children's health and development. She was easy to talk with and clear about her ideas. As a psychologist, she is interested in the entire program and in prevention, not simply in psychodiagnosis and psychotherapy. That sounded good to me.

The three of us examined the children's drawings taped to my walls. We speculated about what they revealed about the emotional state of the artists. It struck us that for the most part they revealed surprisingly little that was worrisome but a great deal about resilience. A girl drew two sailboats floating comfortably on a tranquil sea under a placid sky. A boy drew a delivery truck. Even Anton's tank, bristling with cannons, was at least well conceived and executed. The scenes were generally under control but not obsessively so. They were neither frightening nor chaotic.

Of the drawings that children gave me, it was quiet little Serogia's that caused us the most concern. There were intimations of violence in the way he drew the guns that were his main subject, depression in his use of dark colors, and anxiety in his heavy, repeatedly scored lines.

But over all, the children's artwork would not lead one to imagine that it had been produced by disturbed children. That was remarkable, we thought, in view of what we have come to know of their terrible lives.

We speculated that such lives do not necessarily destroy people. Sometimes those who lead them become very strong as a result.

We talked on until about 10:30. Alla and I were exhausted but Natasha looked as fresh as ever.

- - - - - - - - - - - - - - - -

Vieka begged, "Don't leave, Uncle Bob. Stay another week. *Please!*" It was a sweet thought but she repeated it over and over again *ad nauseum.* "Please, Bob! Please!"

Vieka, twelve, is popular with kids and staff alike, and is also a good athlete. I would have expected whining to be beneath her, but it pleased me to know that she, one of the most together of the kids, wanted me to stay. I had assumed that my constituency was among the most marginal kids, those who are having the hardest time.

- - - - - - - - - - - - - - - -

This morning four kids and I took a final walk around the neighborhood. Participants were Zhenya, Misha—a new boy—Yan, and Dima. We strolled the banks of the River Neva, ran and took many pictures, our usual routine. Tourist boats were tied up at the quay. The crew of one of them invited the children to come aboard and play captain at the steering wheel.

Dima held my hand for almost the whole way there and back. He scolded Yan when he thought he was being too rough with my camera.

Zhenya, twelve, is a sensible, warmhearted girl, obviously intelligent but, I am told, a poor student. The same is true of her eight-year-old sister, Lehrer. I asked Tatiana Igor'ievna why smart children such as these should not be doing well in school.

"Space," she said. "Their family lives in a tiny apartment. Seven children and various relatives are crammed in together.   There is no space for reading or doing homework."

- - - - - - - - - - - - - - - - -

Tatiana—Tanya—Igor'ievna   joined   me   to   the *gastronom*—the grocery story—where I bought ice cream and cake for the kids.   They are throwing a farewell party for me after lunch. We ran into Marina in the store, an intelligent but socially immature girl I knew from last year. It was she who had undergone major heart surgery. Although we were friends then, she didn't recognize me now.

Tanya said that Marina's mother had lost their apartment near Almus.   They now live with acquaintances in another part of the city. Mother has no job. How can they possibly survive? Tanya handed Marina ten rubles—about thirty cents—"for candy."

- - - - - - - - - - - - - - - - -

Irina Ivanovna said, "The children we work with come from terrible families. Their parents drink and beat them. Most families do not have enough to eat. There is much hunger and unhappiness in this neighborhood!"

When you locate a residential program that has the resources to feed children in a neighborhood where parents do not, what happens? What if the program promotes sobriety but the parents are drunks? What if the program is humane but the parents beat their children?

Here is what: Children leave home for the program. Or they are placed by their parents in the program for reasons of survival. In either case, the weak family is further weakened. Or, with good planning and luck, the program becomes a catalyst that triggers transformation of the family and, by so doing, the entire neighborhood.

There are many priutye and dietskiy doma for children without families in this city. Containing them is not a problem unique to Russia. Russia is unusual only in that over the centuries it has developed a generous array of institutions that compensate for family or community deficiencies. These include prisons, summer camps, GULAGs, schools, hospitals, and varieties of orphanages. The trend has recently been accelerated by the increase in poverty and the persistence of the Communist belief that the state can raise a child better than can the family.

Is that true? Is it possible for an institution to be designed to raise a child better than even a marginally adequate family? At once time I didn't believe so but now I wonder. It may be so. I have seen institutions that do indeed strengthen the entire system, the child, the family, and the entire community. Priut Almus, whatever its limitations, is an example.

- - - - - - - - - - - - - - - -

We ate our lunch together. It faded into my farewell party complete with ice cream and cake. We kissed and hugged goodbye. "Please, Uncle Bob, stay just *one* more week," Vieka repeated. Natashinka's kiss was fierce, almost a bite.

- - - - - - - - - - - - - - - -

I am en route to my next adventure, rattling along

by train. I am in a compartment shared with an old woman—probably my age—plus a younger woman and the younger woman's daughter who looks to be nine or ten years old. We have been traveling for almost an hour and a half but have barely spoken at all. It has been established only that I am an American who speaks Russian badly and that they are Russians who speak no English.

- - - - - - - - - - - - - - - - -

Later: Everything has changed. For the past hour, we have been having a fine time. We are friends. The old woman, unrelated to the others, is heading home to Smolensk after having visited her daughter and grandson in St. Petersburg.

The younger woman and the child, Lisa, who is eight, are going to Smolensk to visit Lisa's grandmother. They are from Murmansk where the woman who used to be a teacher is now a travel agent.

Lisa is a sweet child from an intact family. She nonetheless seems much like the priut children with whom I have just spent two weeks. "Bob," she said just as they had, "*Please*, may I play just *one* more game on your computer?" She cuddled up next to me in exactly the way they did. When I shared my dinner with her, she said, "You are a real good guy—*ochen dobryi chelovek*"—in just the same voice as theirs. Lisa kissed me on the cheek when we arrived at her station and we bade each other goodbye. In this she was exactly like Natashinka ... and the others.

- - - - - - - - - - - - - - - - -

Because I have spent so much time with the Priut children, I have tended to attribute their manifest need for physical and emotional closeness to their lives of abuse, deprivation and neglect. But there is something bigger going on here.

What if down-and-out children in this country and those who lead happy lives are just the same? What if the *norm* for children in Russia is to be warm, cooperative, and to trust in the nurturance of adults who in most cases are benign and actually make themselves available emotionally? What if this were true for most people no matter where they live? What if difficult—as distinct from mistreated—children are but a tiny slice of humanity?

2002

Strolling along the Nevsky Prospekt, I saw a drunken teenage boy attempt to hit a Gypsy woman who bravely stood her ground. She was immediately surrounded by three Gypsy men whose very presence kept her tormenter at bay.

I saw a young woman who held a tiny baby on her lap. She squatted on the sidewalk. Beside her was a sign that read, "Help Me for the Love of God." There was a small, wooden icon in front of her with a painting of a bearded saint on it. The woman's head was bowed low so that I could not see her face. She rocked gently to and fro.

I saw a parade of nationalists who held high posters, red banners, and portraits of Lenin and Stalin. They hawked their literature in front of the Gostinny Dvor department store and debated aggressively with passers by. One of the posters read—in English, "Americans! Get Out! Don't You Know That All The World Hates You?"

- - - - - - - - - - - - - - - - -

I know none of the current crop of children but the

vospitatilye and I were pleased to see each other. As is my signature habit, I took many photographs of children and staff. After lunch, I took even more.

The children showed me the new playground in the back yard. It has swings and all sorts of climbing contraptions.

I fall at once into my well practiced and predictable routine. I take pictures. I show them to the children on the camera itself—having long since gone digital. I load them onto the computer and show them off again. Now dozens of children swarm around me and beg me to take their pictures. Again and again and again. I oblige.

I make videos, too. The children are ecstatic, delighted, enthralled. We walk together around the neighborhood. We are friends. We hold hands. We run, skip, and jump. We punch each other on the shoulder. The immature perch on my lap. I give piggy-back rides. I learn their names and ages and a few things about them. The vospitatilye smile approvingly.

Predictable, repetitious ... yet fascinating ... never boring.

There is no study here. It is all play. Why do I do this? Why do I come back for more?

- - - - - - - - - - - - - - - -

Oh, but we must avoid becoming good friends too soon. There are downsides. One is that children such as these are too hungry, too starved for family. They do not need brief encounters with no context, the kind I provide. They require love that lasts. They have experienced too many expectations that lead only to a dulling of the wits and sensibilities.

Real knowledge of the other is a long time a-ripening.

The risk of damage is great if one encourages a child to confound the fleeting with the secure, the false with the true.

- - - - - - - - - - - - - - - - -

In my dotage, I have at long last become a psychologist. I think now in the language of ambience, feeling tone, and morale, and I have learned to disvalue procedures and mechanics. I look to the matrix, the context, and to the child as he or she lives within it.

Where an honest embrace is called for, I provide it, remarking to myself how necessary an embrace is to children such as these. And how fragile they are, how vulnerable they are to betrayal and exploitation.

In the United States, embrace a child and the cry, "Child Abuse!" will be shouted in the streets

But institutions that from fear substitute order for affection, do great harm as well. They create abuse in the name of preventing it. Coldness is abuse. Boundaries can be, too. Professional distance be damned!

I overstate my case. Boundaries are certainly needed. Every role we play requires definition. We must pause and think, make distinctions and choose. I offer myself as Grandpa but not Dad. I love the child but not as lover. Niceties such as these should be self-evident.

The difference between affection and abuse is clear to most of us. But for some few, it is not so simple. I am comfortable when Katinka or Serogia curl up on my lap. With Serogia, affection may also be expressed in a few, short masculine punches or a bear hug. But not with Katinka.

An understanding of the needs of the other is the precondition for having a fine old time together. It must be there at the start of a relationship or nothing good can come of it. Early on, the reality of the other must be in sharp focus.

Returning to Pruit Almus as I have again and again, year after year, is good for me and probably for them, too. Even one-day visits have their value. A relationship between the institution itself and me has been put in place over the years. That relationship continues unacknowledged but is palpably there even with new groups. I have become folklore. I am history. I am part of their world.

- - - - - - - - - - - - - - - -

A final caution: Intimacy has its limits. It must not be permitted to hinder independence and personal growth. There must be a tough, businesslike side to it, marked by high expectations and the confidence that they will be met. Such intimacy grows naturally when working with others and from being together over great chunks of time—if one's head is on straight.

- - - - - - - - - - - - - - - -

Some of the younger boys were hanging around outside as I walked back to Almus after a day of meetings in center city. When they caught sight of me, they pounced and grabbed my hands. "Will you take more pictures?" they asked.

"Take a picture of *me!*"

"Take one of *me* and my friend, *Sasha!*"

I took photographs as requested and showed them around, took a few more and, taking my computer out and asking them to sprawl out comfortably on the floor, I ran Charlie Chaplin's, "The Immigrant," for the crowd. They enjoyed it well enough but it was a beautiful afternoon and games were taking place outside including volleyball and soccer and so after the show, they trotted off the join the others.

The new playground is well equipped with a hand-operated carousel and a sandbox. Because of that, some kids opted out of the movie before it even started.

As they played, I took still more pictures. Then we went inside again to view them. Some stayed for another Chaplin film, *The Adventurer.*

We sprawled on the playroom floor, first with the television set blaring in the background. But the children soon got into Charlie on the computer and someone got up and turned off the TV without even being asked.

Two the boys punched each other for no apparent reason, trading insults at the top of their lungs. One, whose name I did not catch, was the initiator. I told him to bug off. He didn't. I told him to shut up. He wouldn't. I told him to leave the room. He stood his ground. Finally, I shut the computer off thereby stopping the film.

I announced that there would be no movies for anyone unless he would cool it. He finally did.

Natalia Nikolaevna was the vospitatilnitsa on duty. She said, "It is time for uborka but I will give you *ten more minutes* to enjoy the movie."

Uborka is mopping floors and cleaning toilets, not tasks kids take to naturally. But, ten minutes later, the movie was finished and the children went off to attend to their duties without a grumble. Indeed no stress at all was apparent. Perhaps there was even with a touch of willingness in the air.

Oh, I wish I could get action from kids the way these Russian women do. I remain in awe of their power, exercised as it invariably is, with great kindness.

- - - - - - - - - - - - - - - - -

I asked this year's Anya, a well-mannered ten-year-old, how long she had been living at the priut. "I came two days ago," she said. Anya lives nearby, knows some of the children and hopes to go home after a couple of weeks. She is here because her mother needed to go to the hospital for an operation. Anya didn't know exactly what it was for but was aware of its seriousness. Meanwhile, she stays here and her mother knows she is well cared for. "I love Almus," she said.

We should keep in mind that not everyone is in Almus because of parental alcoholism or beatings. Almus is also useful during temporary, stressful setbacks in otherwise okay families.

- - - - - - - - - - - - - - - - -

Priut Almus is a good place. But Makarich's original vision was better, more comprehensive. Makarich set out to provide a family for only a few children at a time, an *ersatz* family where people would stick together, work together and care for each other over generations. But practical necessity got in the way. Almus is now a transitory, less grand thing than its founding dream. It is a life raft, not an ocean liner. Still, it has its uses.

- - - - - - - - - - - - - - - - -

Almus is integral to the larger community but separate from it. Since my last visit, a playground has been built in the back yard. Children from Almus and housing project kids play there when the weather is good as it is today. But there is a downside. Because the playground is on the premises, Almus kids no longer need to walk to playgrounds in the neighborhood.

There is a tendency for all things, notably institutions, to grow until they lose their way and become useless, no longer serving their original purposes or clientele.

- - - - - - - - - - - - - - - - -

"Network" should be the operant word instead of "institution." What if there were a network of semi-autonomous group homes sprinkled about the community, homes of the kind originally intended by Makarich? These might be tied together through a common center and myriad educational, social, political and economic activities and events. Shared resources would be available. The center would be a neighborhood house not unlike what Jane Addams[11] and Lillian D. Wald[12] created in turn-of-twentieth-century America.

Each of these homes would contain a frothy mix of residents. As is now true, some might remain for only a few days while family emergencies are tended to. Others might stay through childhood. Thus there would be various purposes associated with these places along with particular reasons and goals.

Such homes would be led by hard-nosed, idealistic grownups with a capacity for commitment, responsibility, playfulness, even love, all of this accompanied by a determination to involve children in every aspect of planning and administration.

- - - - - - - - - - - - - - - - -

Makarich, the founder and director of Almus, was in his office. He greeted me with his unique mix of intensity, graciousness, warmth and shyness. He is a complex man as I have written, difficult to read. His mission to serve kids is absolute, his ideas are democratic and reasonable. I must interview him.

Makarich looks weary. Life in Russia is hard and his work is draining. There are continual hassles from the authorities that he must deal with, financial worries, responsibility for difficult children, staff issues, anxiety ....

11 *Twenty Years at Hull-House with Autobiographical Notes.* by Jane Addams (1860—1935). New York: The MacMillan Company, 1912 (c.1910).

12 *The House on Henry Street.* Lillian D. Wald's 1915 memoir, H. Holt and Co.

Sure, there are similar contingencies in all of our lives. So it is that we grow older ...

He knows little English and my Russian is as limited. Nonetheless, Makarich launched at once into a long, passionate monologue. I understood no more than an occasional word, enough to guess that he was talking about developments at Almus since I last visited. The fact that little of what he said was getting through to me did not slow him down. He required neither response nor evidence of my agreement. He was formulating his own thoughts more than communicating with me. The discomfort I felt was mine, not his.

"Makarich," I said at last. "Let me show you a collection of photographs of Almus children I have taken over the years. They here on my computer."

I set iPhoto to "slide show" accompanied by selections from Prokofiev's "Aleksandr Nevsky" playing in the background. It was as if strings of particular notes had been planned to coincide with each photograph. Makarich loved it. "Excellent," he said. "Beautiful!" His enthusiasm was infectious. I found myself viewing the pictures with new eyes.

Pictures can substitute for language. Sometimes they are better than words. Mood and relationships caught in a good photograph might not have been conveyed in any other way.

- - - - - - - - - - - - - - - - -

Dinner consisted of kasha, sausages, tea, and fruit compote. I was introduced to the current crop of children none of whom I had known previously. But as a group they looked much like kids who were here in other years. Makarich then took me on a tour of the building to point out changes in program and structure.

In the kitchen of the section of the second floor now housing the older children, a boy and girl were cooking their dinner. "The older children do everything," Makarich explained. "That is how they become prepared for life in the world."

He continued. "This is a community institution," he said. "We have a Drop-in Center for children who want to use it. The residents interact there with those who live at home or on the streets. Our children attend school in the community and come back and forth to their families as needed. They may eventually return home for good, or get adopted or live in a dietskiy dom. We have a close, continuous and flexible relationship with the larger community. In this we are the opposite of traditional orphanages. We do not imprison children. We help them knit relationships in the neighborhood, the city, Russia and the entire world."

(I don't know for sure that he said *every* word exactly as reported above because my Russian is still so entirely *plokho* (bad). But I like to think that he did.)

- - - - - - - - - - - - - - - -

"I played in Uncle Vanya in Vermont last summer," I said.

"What part?" Makarich asked.

"Telegin, also known as 'Waffles,'" I said. I mangled the word, "Waffles," so badly that to a Russian it was probably incomprehensible.

"There is no such character in Uncle Vanya," he said as if that was the final word on the subject.

"There *is!*" I insisted.

Natalia Nikolaevna happened by just then.

"Natalia," I said. "Tell us, who is 'Telegin?'"

"I have no idea," she said.

"A character in Uncle Vanya," I offered. "Waffles."

She left and came back a few minutes later with a copy of Uncle Vanya by A.P. Chekhov. Sure enough, Telegin a.k.a. Waffles, was listed in the cast of characters.

"Only a minor character," she said dismissively.

"What do you mean, 'minor?'" I said. "Chekhov himself wrote that there are no minor characters, only minor players. I take that to apply to theater and all of life."

- - - - - - - - - - - - - - - - -

I ran into Sasha, the geologist vospitatel. "I was looking for you," he said. He led me back into the older kids' kitchen and offered me a seat.

"What can I do for you?"

"Do you know anybody in Alaska?" he asked.

"Alaska? Why Alaska?"

"I have a project in mind for teenagers. St. Petersburg is located between the fifty-ninth and sixtieth parallel north. That is four degrees north of Juno and six degrees south of Fairbanks. If we can find an American group home or orphanage there, we might begin a pen-pal relationship, an educational experience for children in both countries."

"Brilliant!" I said. "I will see what I can find." I researched contacts when I got home and sent them to him.

- - - - - - - - - - - - - - - -

I had a glass of tea with Natalia Nikolaevna and Tatiana Igor'ievna, two of the vospitatilye. They were both well. Tatiana's now fifteen-year-old daughter, Olya, lives in Israel. Mother and child remain very close and miss each other enormously.

Natalia Nikolaevna wore a sporty, white dress edged in red and blue stripes. I wonder if that was in response to a comment I made in an early article to the effect that she seemed "nunlike," a phrase to which she took strong exception. She now looks entirely secular and sporty.

- - - - - - - - - - - - - - - -

Makarich walked Alla Pavlovna and me to the Metro station. The two of them chatted in rapid Russian that I did not even attempt to follow. My mind wandered. We passed an old woman collecting empty bottles from the trash in the street. She placed them in a sack.

"Makarich and I were talking about retirement," Alla explained. "We agreed that when we are old, he and I will collect bottles just like that old woman. Retirement pensions in Russia are worth very little. In a few years they will be worth nothing at all."

- - - - - - - - - - - - - - - -

Outside the Metro station, Alla walked off to buy some apples leaving Makarich and me together.

"Makarich," I asked after a momentary silence, "In your opinion, are current conditions for children in Russia better than they used to be, the same, or worse?"

"In Soviet days," he began, "every detail of life was prescribed. You were required to do this, that, and the other thing. There was no room for thought. Now things are much better in that important respect. Economically, too, there has been some improvement but it has not been so dramatic. Overall, I would say that in the last three years under Putin, the trajectory has been upward for children and almost everyone else.

"With respect to children, I think there are now fewer orphans and semi-orphans and children stay at Almus for a shorter time than they did even a few years ago."

Alla rejoined us. The three of us talked about the differences between how children are treated in America and in Russia. I suggested that Americans are obsessed with control of behavior whereas in Russia children are simply told what to do and do so in the absence of visible reinforcement, positive or negative.

"It is rare," I said, "to see a child punished here."

"You say that," Alla retorted, "because you have only been to nice institutions like Almus. If you saw our terrible places or even our average ones, you would think quite differently. Children are often treated with incredible brutality in this country."

"What you say may be true," I said. "But I am merely highlighting our American preoccupation with control.

You Russians don't talk about it so much. You just go right ahead and control."

"Is it so wonderful to raise children who obey?" she asked, with the classic, ironic smile of the Russian intellectual.

"I didn't say it was. I see it as a mixed blessing," I said.

"How is it mixed?"

"On the one hand," I said, "it is convenient to have children around us who do as they are told. On the other, who needs more passive children in today's unjust world?"

"What interests you about Russia?" Alla asked. "The character of the people?"

"I am interested in your terrible history," I said. "I wonder what its effect has been on character. And I wonder where we Americans would be if we had experienced anything like it."

- - - - - - - - - - - - - - - -

Makarich was waiting for me in front of the Drop-in Center. He wore a welcoming grin. We were joined a moment later by Olga, a nurse I recognized from previous visits. Makarich had arranged for her to bring me to the Center. No more than fifty yards from Almus, it is in a separate building, a crumbling one-story structure surrounded by a forest of cement, high-rise apartment monoliths. Scraps of paper, broken glass vodka bottles and tin cans graced the patches of grass throughout the area. By contrast, inside the center everything was clean and well organized.

A dozen or so adolescents were hanging around. The staff consisted of the young woman director, Alla, a very young vospitatilnitsa whose name I think was Katya, and Lyudmilla, a nurse I recognized from previous visits. Lyudmilla is an indefatigably bubbly person. All three bustled about with the children.

The Vrachi Mira psychiatrist, Dima, arrived with a psychology student in tow. The student's task was to observe Dima administering written tests to several children. Dima is an affable fellow but the test subjects were visibly ill at ease with the entire procedure although none displayed overt resistance.

Much goes on at the center, mostly of a practical sort. Each of the five or six girls in attendance are taking turns in the shower, and fussing afterwards with their hair, excessively so, I thought. Clean clothes were distributed for free and old clothes were washed in the machine. Lyudmilla gave one boy a haircut.

Dima talked with several children and with a woman I assumed to be the mother of one or more of them.

Snacks including cookies, apples and tea were passed around as the television set blared in the back room.

Three boys went outside to roar around on a motorcycle.

At any one time there were perhaps a dozen kids present. But during the two hours I visited, twice to three time that number wandered in and out.

These were residents of this ordinary, very poor neighborhood. Many had rotting teeth. None were

Almus residents but all seemed to feel part of Almus by virtue of its sponsorship of the center.

Deportment throughout was faultless. On request I took a few pictures and showed them to the kids.

Katya, age nineteen, looks much younger and is very thin. "So, you are from America," she said. "America is a very interesting country. I want to go to America someday. But most of all, I want to go to Australia. I want to see kangaroos. I want to travel anywhere.

"Do you love Jesus?" she added suddenly.

"Not particularly," I said.

"Why not?" she asked.

"I am not a Christian."

Katya seemed to accept that answer. No further discussion.

Maxim was the youngest kid in the group. He was eleven and seemed at loose ends. Lyudmilla, the nurse, gave him a huge hug. "Maxim is an excellent boy," she said.

I talked with Dima, the Vrachi Mira psychiatrist. He described the work he does at the center but the words flowed out of him so quickly and with such detail that I soon lost the thread. "Speak slowly, Dima," I begged. "I can't understand you unless you speak very, very slowly."

What I was able to glean is that Dima does a great many things including psychotherapy and problem-solving through doll-play, a non-threatening version of psychodrama.   He also works with entire families as necessary.

During our conversation, several teen age girls hurried by. One of them stopped for a moment to give Dima a peck on the cheek.

When the session ended, everyone left without a fuss but it felt as though they would have been glad to move right into the center if allowed to do so.

I appreciated the mood, the informality and the focus on responding to the practical needs of neighborhood children including the very poorest among them.

Priut Almus is more than a children's shelter. It is a multi-service center benefitting the entire community.

- - - - - - - - - - - - - - - -

"Why don't you allow children to spend the night here," I asked Makarich afterwards.

 "No funding," he said.

2005

This time I am in Russia on a different errand. I am a consultant to an organization that has brought fifteen American adolescents here to work in a boarding school, not Almus. But I thought I would visit Almus briefly to see how things are going. I am not interested so much in Almus itself as in the Drop-in Center. I wanted to learn more about how it functions. The Center is affiliated with the priut and sponsored by Vrachi Mira. I saw it for the first time on my last trip to Russia.

In the interim, a security protocol has been adopted. To gain admission, one must first knock on the steel front door. I did so. It was soon opened by two women staff members whom I did not know. They welcomed me in nonetheless.

I told them who I was, something of my prior work with Almus, and of my interest in the Center. They asked me to sit down and make myself comfortable. The children would be arriving in about an hour, they said.

A young woman showed up some minutes later. She introduced herself as Becky Bavinger, an American student from Georgetown University here on an internship as part of her undergraduate Russian studies program. Becky had studied the Russian language in college. She works at the drop in center as a coordinator in addition to her translator job in the Vrachi Mira office. With all that experience, her mastery of the Russian language sounded quite complete—at least to my faulted ear.

Becky offered me tea as we discussed her work and mine. I thought it curious that she had thus far not visited Priut Almus itself despite working in the Drop-in Center, a stone's throw away. The two institutions are apparently more discrete than I had supposed.

I walked with her to the Almus building where I introduced her to Makarich. Then I gave her a tour of the facility explaining the program as well as I could while doing so.

When we returned to the Center, we found that a half-dozen kids had arrived, one of whom, Carina, recognized me from my previous visit. I recalled that last time she had refused to let me take her photograph.

Another girl, Nastia, was busy applying make-up to her face. Three boys and one girl played checkers and two girls, cards. A staff member gave a haircut to a boy.

Local kids, many of them homeless, drop in to the Center for showers and an occasional meal. They are offered medical help, counseling, friends, games, leads to jobs, and a place to nap—but there are no facilities to sleep overnight. A girl, snoring on a sofa, stirred. A CD player spewed forth Russian rock but not so loudly as to awaken her.

The Drop-in Center is housed in an undistinguished,

cement block and white-brick structure in the midst of a similarly styled housing project, late Soviet period, not very old but the facade is crumbling and the white bricks cry for a deep cleaning.

In Russia, public places that I have seen, including the grounds of housing developments, tend to be ignored. Grass is not mowed, sidewalks are cracked, and when it rains, you cannot walk from one door to the next without getting mud on your shoes. Trash proliferates. But the apartments themselves in such projects, where people actually live, are often spotless. Everything in the home tends to be in its place in spite of painfully cramped quarters.

A girl, sitting by herself, half-smiled in my direction. Her name, she said, was Olya. She had the olive skin of a Gypsy. She told me that she was eighteen but looked younger. She was thin and had bruises on her arm and face. I asked if I could take her photograph. "Please do," she said. I did. Then she wanted me to take another one, this time with a young woman volunteer from Poland, Hagar, whose last name I do not recall.

I was eager to learn Olya's story but felt uncomfortable to ask because it was likely to be a painful one and Becky, who might have advised me and translated, was busy in the kitchen.

One of the staff members organized games beginning with musical chairs. Some involved dancing and some called for singing, all uncool by international teenage standards but these rugged children of the streets enjoyed themselves immensely.

A spaghetti dinner was served followed by a birthday party complete with ice cream and cake. Unfortunately,

I was accompanying a bunch of American teenagers on another project and needed to depart too early for the party. Worse, I never got to meet the birthday boy. I am not even sure which one he was.

I whispered goodbye to Becky and Hagar and took my leave as unobtrusively as I could.

- - - - - - - - - - - - - - - - -

(Oh, someday I will return. I promise to remain in Russia for a year or more, learn the language, live in Almus, and volunteer my services at the Drop-in Center.)

- - - - - - - - - - - - - - - -

The Center is a good place to learn about children such as these, the flotsam and jetsam of society, but as an institution it is faulted. It cannot possibly meet the infinite needs of its target population. These kids have neither family, money, education, jobs, clothes, food, nor stability; they have prison records and are drug and alcohol dependent; they die in the streets of AIDS and drug-resistant tuberculosis. They have no institutional surcease, no pruit, no internat, no dietskiy dom. Russia does not talk about them. The world does not hear of them.

All that the Drop-in-Center provides is not sufficient to make a critical difference.

How many crippled lives can be remedied by a program that doesn't offer so much as an overnight bed? By a program that is only open from three in the afternoon to eight in the evening and not at all on weekends? ...And is not a home.

The staff consists of wonderful people who do their best, but they work with minimal resources, financial and otherwise.

- - - - - - - - - - - - - - - -

Makarich's ideas are romantically antiauthoritarian and include summer camps in the country near rivers and lakes. The entire Almus enterprise is built on a human scale with a focus on the individual in the context of family, the neighborhood and the larger society.

My own antiauthoritarianism may come from being an only child. Makarich's was likely grown in an orphanage. Scars remain. Everyone's childhood leaves its marks through succeeding generations. Personal histories may be a guide to fashion tools to change the world.

Anybody can change the world but who among us can change it for the better?

- - - - - - - - - - - - - - - -

Makarich and I chatted amiably without benefit of translator yet with a surprising degree of comprehension. He said that the residential program is going along as well as ever but that the numbers are down because of the increasing use of the new Almus foster child program. Children no longer require a priut so much these days.

Reaching for my best Russian, I struggled to say that the temporary residence model may nonetheless be the more helpful one for most children. Foster care is not for everyone, neither is adoption, and incarceration in an institution of any kind should be beyond the pale for civilized society. But offering a short term, flexible, familial, community-based home may be the most useful gift to young people who, against all odds, struggle to grow up sane and healthy in a less than perfect world.

2008

I am in St. Petersburg yet again. My agenda is to finish this book. I am sitting in Makarich's office waiting for him. I *will* interview the guy. After all these years, I have not been able to do so properly. He is now willing and is off to find us a translator.

His three secretaries are working ... well, one is reading a book, but the other two are definitely hard at work, one on a computer and the other, writing on paper. Yes, there is a computer in this office as well as a copy machine and three telephones—two landline and one cell. Where is the antique Almus I knew of old?

Makarich is a man of the theater. How does he use theater in his work with children? I have come to believe that work with children *is* theater. There are roles to be played, information and skills to be conveyed but what is essential is how characters relate to each another. This is true as well in the works of Anton Chekhov, in whose plays both Makarich and I have acted. What is key for Chekhov, Makarich and me is neither content, style, plot nor character alone but ambience and the human interactions that may be understood only in context.

- - - - - - - - - - - - - - - -

Svetlana Konstantinova, "Sveta," our translator, is a cultured, self-contained woman who has a lot to say in her own voice. But she is a disciplined professional— woman of the theater and teacher of English—and did not permit her personal views to interrupt the flow of our conversation.

As a child, Sveta had acted in the Leningrad Children's Theater under Makarich's direction.

"He is a very great man," she said.

- - - - - - - - - - - - - - - -

Makarich arrives, bustling, speaking rapidly, forcefully and with artful use of his hands. He addresses first the office staff and then Sveta and me. He is in high spirits and, unlike other people I know, appears actually younger than he did two years ago when I last saw him.

The History of Priut Almus

An interview with

Mikhail Makarievich, Founder/Director

Svetlana Konstantinova, Translator

May 21, 2008

We founded Almus in 1991 just after the collapse of the Soviet Union. The situation in St. Petersburg—and throughout Russia—was very bad then. The political collapse led to severe difficulties in the financial sector and, beyond that, in the family. There was a sudden increase in deep poverty especially as it impinged on the upbringing of children.

Local authorities were open to ideas then about how to solve these problems. They were particularly interested in creating a system to protect the rights of children. A network of experimental institutions and organizations emerged for that purpose.

Only dietskiy doma and internatye existed before that. Dietskiy doma are similar to orphanages as they once were found throughout Europe and America. Internatye are public boarding schools, more open to the community than dietskiy doma. Their residents are not necessarily orphans or children at risk. But both are formal institutions and as such present many impediments to familylike child care, not the least of which is that they require considerable legal paperwork before a child may be admitted. Termination of parental rights is a precondition.

These rights are transferred to the city government that then places the child in an institution selected by the authorities. A child may not be admitted at his or her own request and has no say in the choice of placement. It is therefore clear that such places cannot serve as a refuge from abuse or neglect as defined by the child him or her self according to his or her own perceptions and experiences. A less drastic, less formal, more flexible structure was missing.

Before there were priutye, children were simply picked up off the streets by the police and their fate was determined by the same officers. It was our sense, mine and that of my colleagues, that in a democratic society, police should not be the ones to make such decisions. Was it right, we asked, for a child to be placed in a total institution simply on the word of a police man or woman? Was it proper for parents to lose their rights without going through a court process? These realizations were central to the thinking of those of us who were bent on creating a new and better system for the protection of children.

A dietskiy priut—a shelter for children—was the model we turned to. The form had existed prior to the Revolution but during Soviet times, it had been abandoned. What is distinctive about a priut is that a child may be admitted at his or her own request thus greatly empowering the individual child. At the same time, there are no negative consequences for parents. Their rights could remain intact. The arrangement is consistent with the ancient Russian tradition that a child should have a favored status in society even if he or she happens to be an orphan, or an abandoned, abused or neglected minor.

Funding was a problem from the start. On the one hand, federal, regional and city governments are obliged to spend money to deal with children at risk. But the fact is that in the early 1990s, the governments had neither the funds nor the will. They had other priorities. Police filled the vacuum and took responsibility.

While it is true that shelters and group homes for children have existed in the West for some time, it may be that Almus is different from them in some significant respects that I am not aware of.

Priut Almus grew from my own history and experiences. As a child, I lived in a dietskiy dom. It was not a bad place. I have many good memories of it. Best of all, it was located right in the middle of Leningrad in the Smolny District, an historic, well-favored neighborhood,. The high culture of the city surrounded us and, as luck would have it, my dietskiy dom did not have its own school but rather sent us to the local district school that happened to be one of the best in the city. There we received a real eduction.

Most other dietskiy doma residents were not so fortunate. There is normally little of educational value that exists beyond the walls of most institutions for children. Residents sit alone with their problems and have no prospect of being exposed to culture, the outdoors, the life of the mind, the imagination, or any resources at all that might lead them to a life beyond their sadness

The government supported our dietskiy dom and the district school with the required necessities including food, clothes and so on. But resources overall were extremely limited at the time. There were no extras. This, you see, was immediately after the Second World War. Yet somehow funds were found to send us to camp each summer. The government did as well by us as it could. At the same time, we were deprived of those less tangible things that are necessary for every child, a real home and the realization that somebody needs you and that you need them.

Some of us found ways to compensate. We discovered that on our own initiative we could become engaged in interesting after-school activities. Our city had a great deal to offer even during that difficult time. I myself was drawn to theater. I came to love theater passionately. It became my salvation.

Memories of my childhood, despite living in an institution, are rather pleasant. In some ways I had a rich, emotionally satisfying, life. For example, my dietskiy dom did not prevent me from attending a neighborhood theater club. I am forever grateful for having had such an opportunity. Many children experience nothing similar.

In Almus, children are given as much cultural exposure as we can provide. We take them to museums, concerts, the circus, and all manner of cultural events.

The saddest times I remember in the dietskiy dom were the so-called Parent Days when children were allowed to visit with their relatives, whether grandparents, aunts and uncles, and, if they had them, mothers and fathers. These took place on weekends, holidays or vacations.

Not all children were fortunate enough to have somebody come for them. The most terrible feeling is the loneliness, the sense of being neglected. On Parent Days you stood by a very tall window looking out at the street below, waiting, waiting, waiting for someone to come, someone who would take you with them. But no one comes. I can still remember that desperate loneliness.

Can you imagine a still worse scenario—a child who not only has no one but also has no hobby to compensate, no favorite thing to do, no experiences to draw on, nothing to read, nothing to stimulate the imagination, no way to escape? It is dreadful. Such a child will have problems for his or her entire life.

That image of the child by the window has haunted me for years. During Soviet times, such a child had only the possibility of a dietskiy dom or an internat but today there are other resources. Children who watch at the window now might be welcomed into foster families, group homes, priutye, and so on. At Almus, we offer children as many interesting activities as we can, the possibility of choice and the likelihood of being treated as a person, as an individual human being.

Another significant problem with traditional institutions for children in our country is that vospitatilye work a series of eight hour shifts. There is little chance in such an arrangement that a particular child will become attached to a particular adult. It is a system designed to make surrogate parenting unlikely.

But here, too, we at Almus do things differently. We

assign a fixed number of children, usually six or seven, to each vospitatilnitsa. And each vospitatilnitsa works two twenty-four hour shifts per week. During that period, she is fully present with responsibility for those particular children. And the children appreciate it. While not perfect, this system greatly increases personal contact and commitment. It approximates parenthood.

Before Almus, I was a vospitatel in a dietskiy dom. I was given considerable autonomy. For a year I experimented with the staffing arrangement to demonstrate that it is best to work twenty-four-hour shifts and bear responsibility for a specific, limited number of children. At one point I worked with another vospitatel and for one entire week the two of us took care of specific children alone. They were our responsibility. Sure enough, the children became quieter and more manageable under this regime. In fact, they even came to respect us as human beings and vospitatilye, a rare occurrence in such a place.

I remember once when I was taking a nap, the children returned from a day in school. They opened the door and saw me. I heard them whisper, "Shhh! Shhh! Don't shout. Makarich is sleeping!"

It is unheard of in dietskiy doma to speak with such respect and kindness about a vospitatel. On the contrary, children in such places love to tease vospitatilye and take every opportunity to give them a hard time. But under our system, a climate of human respect was generated.

Our unit constituted one-sixth of that dietskiy dom and fortunately we were granted permission to remain almost entirely independent of the main unit. One of our best innovations was for the children to be given their own kitchen where they could take tea, eat a snack, or just sit and talk when they wished to. They soon came to respect all of their surroundings, the entire milieu.

Unfortunately, there was no possibility at that time for us to teach them how to use money. We had none to offer. But three years ago, we at Almus received a grant from the Lenin Fund and for the first time were able to give the children such an opportunity. We initiated the unusual practice of giving children pocket money.

Children who live in institutions normally have no opportunity to learn the most rudimentary routines of life that the rest of us take for granted, budgeting, shopping, cooking, planning the day, making decisions, and setting personal goals.

My background is not pedagogy. It is theater. It was my own first theater director who was my best teacher. It was he who had the greatest influence on me. He created such a tight group that every one of us on waking in the morning could not wait to be on stage under his direction.

Our second performance was Tom Sawyer. Through Tom Sawyer, our director introduced me to a world that I had not imagined before. We were exposed to American music and were shown photographs of America. This man gave us a sense of entirely different ways of being.

I remember when I myself became a director and we did The Little Prince, *we rehearsed until four in the morning but the next day at seven in the evening we were to be on stage for the performance. We managed to get there but the performance failed. Yet nobody left the troupe, everyone remained. They scolded me for the failure of this performance. But nobody quit. Everyone stayed and continued to respect my leadership.*

In general, I think it is personality that is of greatest importance in working with children, not pedagogy but personality, especially the personality of the director. The work itself is like theater. You organize your troupe. You deal each day with new circumstances. You constantly confront new tasks and superordinate tasks.

The 8 of March is Women's Day in Russia. The men who work in the priut with the children put on a show that day for the women on staff. Once we rented four different film productions of Shakespeare's Romeo and Juliet. We saw the play performed by four different Juliets and four different Romeos. This was not done to compare the versions but to give the children an opportunity to see a variety of high level interpretations of the same play.

It was a powerful lesson. Afterwards, some of the girls decided not to go into careers in acting because they could imagine themselves playing Juliet and concluded that they had insufficient talent. But the theatrical experience allowed the children to learn about themselves through becoming different characters.

But I have come to believe that combining Almus children with theater is impossible. Theater demands a high level of intellectual development. Unfortunately, most of my children are far below this level. To allow them to perform without the maturity they require will mean that the performance will not be interesting to an audience. I want my theater to be up to the mark. To offer second-rate theater is not for me.

My best theater group was at the Pioneer Youth Palace years ago. We did have such things during Soviet times. The children attended the group over a period of eight years, time enough for them to develop.

One of the problems in Almus is that the children come and go. There are often only a few very talented children here with whom you can make a good production and they remain with us for a very short time. A priut is not allowed by law to house a child for more than one year. After that, he or she must either return home, be adopted, sent to a foster family, or enter a dietskiy dom or an internat. This makes theater productions at Almus quite unlikely because of the time required for training, set design, rehearsal and performance.

I remember one boy we had who was an excellent actor. He could even play the Little Prince. But he stayed with us for only four months.

We have children who remain in the area after they leave, but we have many more who, when they enter into a new family, whether foster or adoptive, want to cut off all ties with their previous life. For example, a vospitatilnitsa needed to do a home visit to prepare a report on the birth parents. She suggested that the child come along with her but he refused, saying, "No! I am afraid you are going to leave me there!" It takes a long time for a child to learn that they can calm down and trust us.

It is very difficult to predict the future of Almus. My dream is to provide a life for children that would be centered in an apartment. We had such a project in mind when we began but it was not supported financially.

Sometimes it takes as long as two years to implement

a project and to sign off on all the necessary papers. During that time, the city and province do provide some money but it is usually too little, enough perhaps to make a few cosmetic renovations but not enough for construction. So, when you finally come back to the government with the necessary papers in hand, signed, you discover that the money has already been spent or is committed elsewhere.

Almus is supported by the city and provincial governments. We do not look for grants from non governmental organizations or foundations.

For our future, I would very much like to implement a "social flats" idea. This is my current dream. I would like to have nothing but an office in the building that we now occupy. I would take all the children away and set them up them in apartments. With such an arrangement, the life of a child would closely approximate that in a normal family. They would live with roommates, attend school, and, when necessary, go to a polyclinic. Money is, of course, a huge impediment.

We now have twenty-four children living in the priut itself plus sixteen who are in family group homes. Ten are in the day care center. We have six in "social observation." The Drop-in Center? I can't say how many are there at any given time. It varies from day to day.

Unfortunately, we do not have the resources to do follow-up studies. We do not have sufficient contact with alumni. For the most part, we don't know where they are, or what or how they are doing.

Now you must excuse me. I must answer the telephone in the next room.

- - - - - - - - - - - - - - - -

Some months later, after the interview was translated and transcribed, I responded,

- - - - - - - - - - - - - - - -

Makarich, my friend,

Thank you for the remarkable interview. It provided me with valuable background on Priut Almus but it also raised some issues that beg for further consideration. I want to take a moment to begin that process.

What a pity it would be if you were to give up the residence in favor of foster homes! I beg you to resist the temptation to do so. Although something is surely gained in a foster home in that a child is likely to get more personal attention, much is also lost. A residence provides rich, group dynamics and the possibility of generating programs that can offer powerful social learning experiences.

Theater offered such gifts to you. Almus in turn passes them on to the many children who came through here over the years.

While it is true that foster homes can provide a good life for a child especially if there are several children there at once, more often foster care is a lonely proposition where closeness is stifling and personalities are incompatible. Abuse is a constant, ominous danger, supervision is difficult, accountability negligent and the child is deprived of the vital cacophony of a larger community.

I can readily understand that a Russian adult, having

lived through the era of compulsory community, may view a turn toward the individual to be attractive. But many of us who have suffered the extreme individualism of the American experience often feel similarly drawn to the possibilities of the group, the healthy group, the voluntary association, the liberating group as distinct from the prison, the army, the orphanage, or the komunalka.

It is not a question of one or the other. A balance is possible. It is the individual within the group who most interests me, not the one in opposition to it. You have already discovered a sound formula in Almus. But I am concerned that you may be tempted to abandon it for the American way. Surely you will proceed with the utmost caution.

On another matter: What is this about limiting participation in theater to the talented? If that policy had been in place here in Vermont, I would never have stepped on the stage thus depriving friends and neighbors of my cameo appearances. Why must all worthwhile theater be professional? What about community theater? And theater as a way of learning about life? Or theater as literature? Or theater as social criticism? Or theater as a vehicle for trying out new ways of being? Or theater as a showcase for the exploration of future goals and possibilities?

What if Almus were to become both a residence and a school of theater arts—not simply for the talented but for all those who have a story to tell, whether wonderful or terrible.

Each child would be encouraged to share his or her story upon entering such a priut. The story would be told and retold, written, declaimed, and performed with the assistance of friends and recorded in photographs, MP3 files, and videos.

It would tie the past of the child together with the present and ultimately project his or her imagination into a positive future. On departing Almus, each child would be presented with a tangible record of his or her life and possibilities.

Why not go still further?   Why not make Almus a center not only of theater but of all the arts—music, dance, literature, painting, gardening, architecture, film, photography, indeed of any modality that permits personal expression and recognition?

Almus has taken a major step in that direction insofar as children are brought regularly to theaters, museums, and concert halls. I am suggesting a second step in which the child would be transformed from spectator, consumer of the arts, to producer and artist whether in the service of his or her own development or for an audience of friends. or the general public and posterity.

Why not?

Almus stands already as a monument to spirited and humane ways to raise children who are in need.

If you will permit me one more comment: You claim not to be conversant with the literature of pedagogy. You say that your field is simply theater and it is from theater that Almus has evolved. Yet I cannot help but hear the echos and note the commonalities between what you have achieved and the best endeavors over recent centuries by progressive educators from Russia, Europe and the United States.   The tradition includes

Jean-Jacques Rousseau,[13] *Friedrich Froebel,*[14] *Johann Pestalozzi,*[15] *Leo Tolstoy,*[16] *Lev Vigotsky,*[17] *John Dewey,*[18] *Maria Montessori,*[19] *Janusz Korczak,*[20] *Jean Piaget,*[21] *Rudoph Steiner,*[22] *Paolo Friere,*[23] *and countless others.*

What such people have in common is the idea of the child as active learner. Far more than digesting prior wisdom, he or she is able to construct the world anew. Over the centuries, this remains a revolutionary idea, forged in practice, a concept particularly well suited to work with children such as those in Priut Almus and its various programs.

---

13 Rousseau, Jean-Jacques Rousseau. *Emile, or On Education.* Trans. Allan Bloom. New York: Basic Books, 1979.

14 http://core.roehampton.ac.uk/digital/froarc/frochi/.

15 Silber, Kate. *Pestalozzi: The Man and his Work.* London: Routledge and Kegan Paul, 1960.

16 *Tolstoy as Teacher: Leo Tolstoy's Writings on Education* by Leo Tolstoy; Bob Blaisdell; Christopher Edgar. *Comparative Education Review*, Vol. 44, No. 4 (Nov., 2000).

17 Van der Veer, Rene (2007). *Lev Vygotsky: Continuum Library of Educational Thought.* Continuum.

18 http://www.gutenberg.org/etext/852.

19 O'Donnell, Marion (2007). *Maria Montessori: Continuum Library of Educational Thought.* Continuum.

20 Lifton, Betty Jean (1988). *The King of Children: A Biography of Janusz Korczak.* Harper Collins.

21 Piaget, J., and Inhelder, B. (1962). *The Psychology of the Child.* New York: Basic Books.

22 Hemleben, Johannes and Twyman,Leo, *Rudolf Steiner: An Illustrated Biography.* Rudolf Steiner Press, 2001.

23 http://marxists.anu.edu.au/subject/education/freire/pedagogy/index.htm.

A proper discussion of this topic is beyond the scope of this book. But can you not feel the first, early tremors of a conference coming on?

Thank you for providing me the opportunity to know Priut Almus in action and to have apprenticed myself to you, your staff, and your children, each person an unique and valuable mentor.

I hope to drop in again next time I am in St. Petersburg as I hope someday to show you around Vermont. We have a comfortable guest room in our home that awaits you.

Sincerely,

Bob

End Note

Dr. Roman Yorick, director of Doctors of the World, St. Petersburg, sent me an email today, November 7, 2008, that read in part,

"Mikhail Makarievich was quite hastily and unhappily retired by the authorities a couple of weeks ago."

Portraits

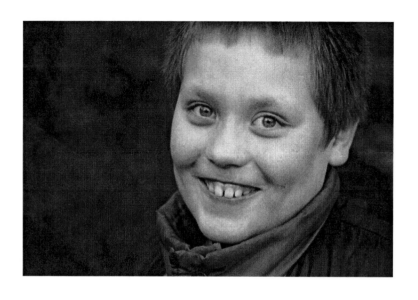

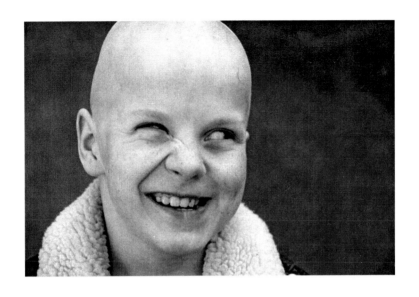

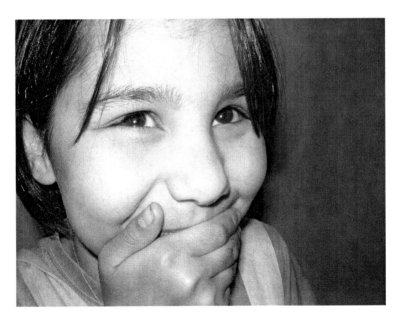

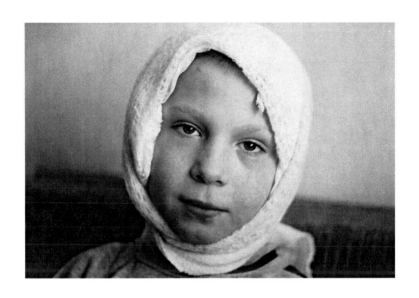

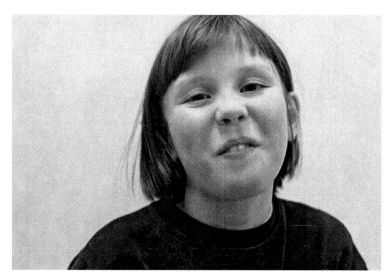

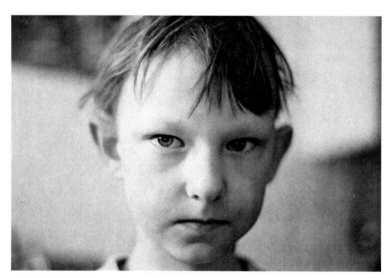

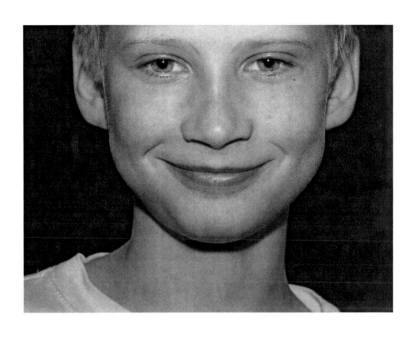

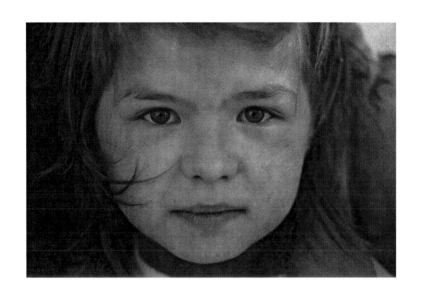

Appendix

In this study, we have often used items from the following interview schedule.[24] It's purpose was to generate the flow of conversation, not to arrive at a diagnosis. Only a few of the questions, varying according to the perceived needs of the child, were used at a time and were selected on the spot. We occasionally changed the wording to insure comprehension. New questions were invented and added freely as we thought of them.

What is your name? What do you prefer to be called? Why?
How old are you? What age would you most like to be? Why?

- **Pretend to look into a mirror and tell us what you see.**

- **Finish this sentence: I remember ...**

- **How have you changed since you were little? How are you different now? Why do you think you have changed? How are you unlike other people? How are you the same?**

---
24 We used a Russian translation.

- Where do you live? What's it like there? Where did you live before? What was it like?

- Do you go to school? If not, do you want to? Explain. What grade are you in? What stands out for you in school? What's best about your experience? What's worst? Explain.

- Do you work? What do you do? What's it like? What work would you want to do someday?

- What are your interests, your hobbies?

- Finish this sentence: It's too bad that ...

- Looking over your whole life so far, what stands out for you? What has been important? What stories come to mind?

- Whom do you call "family"? What are they like? Will you have your own family some day? Why or why not?

- What about your friends. What are they like?

- How do you spend a typical day?

- Finish this sentence: When I ...

- What makes you happiest?

- What makes you saddest?

- What makes you angriest?

- What are your dreams?

- What are you working on in your self or your life?

- What do you want? For yourself? For others?

- If you were President, what would be your program and why?

- If you were super rich, what would you do with your money?

- If you were on television and everyone in the world were watching, what would you do? What would you say?

- What do you see in your future? What do you imagine you'll be doing in ten years? Twenty? What would you like to be doing?

- When you die, what do you imagine people might say about you?

Printed in the United States
216148BV00004B/1/P